Brave

Britney Buckwalter

D1714533

Carol
Thank you for Being a
Part of my Tribe!

Love Always

Cover Photo By: Pamela Hoth

https://pamelamichellephotography.com/

Edited By: Teja Rhae Watson

https://www.tejarhae.com/

FIRST EDITION: October 18th, 2023

ISBN:9798864500712

Imprint: Independently Published

Contents

This Book Is Dedicated To

Barbara Jean Case

"We are so lightly here; it is in love that we are made and in love we disappear" - Leonard Cohen

Acknowledgments

To my moon and my sun, my guiding lights: London, my beautiful daughter, and Ledger, my handsome son. May your mother's story (once you are old enough to read it) inspire you to find a path in life that makes you as happy as you have made me. Always be WHO YOU ARE, nothing more and nothing less. Never forget that my love for you is limitless, and always remember what a gift you are to this world. Thank you for inspiring me to be a better version of myself every day. I love you more than life itself.

To Mathew, thank you for supporting my ever-changing and evolving lifestyle, and for the abundance of love you have brought into my life. Thank you for showing me what support and absolute devotion looks like. The patience, loyalty, and respect you have shown me, made me believe in love again. I am forever grateful for you, Brantley, and Violet. I love you so very much, my North Star. You hold my heart always.

To my family, my roots. My Mother, Cheryl—thank you for so fiercely supporting me in the many directions my life has taken, and for never giving up on me. Thank you for being an endless source of love and leadership, even when it wasn't easy. To Ron, my stepfather, thank you for believing in me. Without your interest and support so early on in my career as an intuitive and medium, I would not have had the confidence or courage to do what I do today. I am forever grateful for you and our many talks.

To my father John, thank you for showing me what good work ethic and morals are, thank you for the time and dedication you've put into raising me, and for all the guidance you've given me over the years. Thank you for choosing to love me—I am who I am today because of you. To my father Keith, your tireless determination and dedication to your family inspires me every day. I hope one day I can be as gentle, kind, and helpful to others as you have been to everyone you know.

To Grammy—thank you for constant love, support, humor, and help with the children, throughout this process. I am forever grateful for the relationship we have today.

To my second parents, Pat and Bill Kerns, thank you for speaking my language, for being my number-one fans, and for all the moments and words of divine wisdom you have shared with me. Thadd, Liza, and I are forever grateful for you.

And to the people who inspired me the most: my tribe. My beautiful bounty of friends that are family to me. To Holly and Ken Woodruff, thank you for the push. Thank you for opening up my eyes and being my rock during those early years. Cassie and Chris Smith, and Megan Krigbaum, thank you for all your help with events, our many talks, and your love and support.

To Chantelle Renee Courville & Sherri Perry for believing in me, for all of our long talks, and the deep, divine guidance you have shared with me over the years. You are the most inspiring women in my life, and I am forever grateful for you, my sisters. Thank you for holding my hand through the hard times.

To my editor Teja Watson, thank you for your many hours of patience and dedication throughout this process. Without you this book would not have been possible!

To my guides, Spirit, and the ascended masters that put up with me: thank you for the opportunity to serve you, it is a true honor. Thank you for your constant guidance and support. I love you.

And most importantly: to you, the reader. Thank you for your belief and interest in mediumship, psychic science, and my story. Thank you for your support. Without you, this wouldn't be possible! I love you, ROCK ON!

Introduction

I wanted to write this book for my amazing followers (that would be you) who struggle to find and/or have yet to step into their purpose in life. It is my hope that this book inspires whoever holds it in their hands (or listens to it) to take whatever steps necessary to finally invest in yourself! Remember, comfort is a beautiful garden to sit in, but nothing ever grows there....

There are six types of bravery, and I would like to share them with you before we begin:

Physical Bravery: Not letting anything or anyone get in your way, moving forward no matter how hard it might be, while maintaining focus and balance.

Social Bravery: The ability to be your true genuine self in social situations, both publicly and online, the ability to be completely and totally, unapologetically you.

Moral Bravery: Simply doing the right thing, no matter how you may look to others while doing it.

Emotional Bravery: Allowing yourself to feel all of your emotions, even if someone belittles you for doing so. Acknowledging those feelings without guilt.

Intellectual Bravery: Leading your life with an open mind at all times, understanding that we will be learning until the end of our days, that no one knows everything, and that we are all students of the Universe. Willing to adapt to new knowledge at all times.

Spiritual Bravery: Finding your soul's purpose on Earth and living it out with kindness, patience, and acceptance—not just for yourself, but toward all living things.

I challenge you to identify all six types of bravery within this book—I promise they are there. Before we begin, here's a bit on the lingo. In this book I have chosen, out of respect, to capitalize "Spirit" when I am referring to the collective whole. I will lowercase "spirit" when I am referring to "a" or "the" spirit. It's also important for you to know the difference between guides and Spirit.

While your guides are in spirit, they are not who I am referring to when I say "Spirit." I am using "Spirit" in the same way I would use the word "people" to describe humankind. A guide, on the other hand, is a person, now in spirit, who has lived many former lives on Earth, has paid all of their karmic debts, and no longer needs to reincarnate; they have been promoted to assisting others on their spiritual journey. Interesting tidbit for you, it is believed by many (myself included) that we choose our guides while in the spirit realm, before we are born and/or reincarnate.

Now, with that being said, here is your warning, this book isn't for the faint of heart or easily offended. I don't know why "fuck" flies so freely from my mouth (that's not true, it is the fault of my Mother, Cheryl, and my Aunt Lana), but it does, along with many other inappropriate, magically descriptive words. If this is something you cannot handle, please close this book and immediately give it to the coolest person you know.

Part One

Chapter 1

Trust

If there is one thing I'm sure of, it's Spirit's ability to make shit happen! It doesn't matter what you need—more money, more love, more support, a new job—just ask and you shall receive. You just have to have some patience, and an abundance of trust, and they will come through for you.

By early 2017, it was clear to me, through each reading I conducted, that I was becoming a professional intuitive and medium. With each reading I carried out, I began to feel a push to take my training (nearly all of which came from books and my own experiences) to the next level. I wanted to work with respected, experienced platform mediumship teachers who poured passion into their curriculum.

I started to research the top mediumship and psychic workshops offered in the US. I kept looking, until I felt intuitively drawn to the right program and teachers. After nearly a week of research, I had finally found a program that suited me—the only problem was, it was literally on the other side of the country and would cost me at least two grand. I didn't have an extra two thousand bucks just lying around, so I closed my computer and went on about my day, thinking, "Eh, it will happen if it's supposed to happen."

The next morning, I woke up thinking about a really strange word: *LaPlata*. I wasn't even sure how to spell this word—it sounded French to me. So, I did what any person in my shoes would do...I Googled it! It turned out to be the name of a tiny little town here in Missouri, a little over an hour from Hannibal. *LaPlata,* I kept hearing it...*LaPlata, LaPlata.* A town of less than thirteen hundred people that was located in Macon County.

There was a small venue hall in LaPlata called "The Depot Inn." I looked at the pictures of this train-themed hotel and conference center and felt that push I so heavily rely on to guide me. I was worried that such a small community would have very little interest in mediumship, as I was from a little town, a town where the nearest metaphysical event was nearly two hours south.

Then it hit me: I would've given anything to have grown up in a place where mediumship and psychic science seekers had a supportive community. So, I called the depot, paid for the space, and got to creating the event on social media.

I posted it on my public Facebook page (with only about 200 followers at the time): "There will be a Mediumship Demonstration in LaPlata Missouri, ticket link below!" At this point in time (2018), I was still very new to the world of platform mediumship. As far as audience attendance went, I think the biggest group I had ever read was ten, maybe twelve people.

Within 24 hours the room I had purchased (which would fit up to thirty people) had suddenly become too small! The event was completely sold out, and I was getting messages asking if there was any chance there might be a second event that day, or if more tickets would be on sale; people were asking to be put on a wait list. I scheduled a second demonstration for later that day and again it sold out almost immediately!

When I realized that the amount I had made in less than forty-eight hours would allow me to take the classes I felt drawn to, I was humbled. I felt so small— which is funny, you would think one would feel special, like some kind of big deal, but this phenomenon had the opposite effect on me. An overwhelming feeling of gratitude washed over me. I got on my hands and knees and said, "Thank you for proving to me that I am not alone on this journey, thank you, thank you, thank you." I had made enough money to cover training fees for the classes, my plane tickets out east, a rental car, a hotel, and food! Before booking my plane tickets and paying for the class, I remember sitting at the edge of my bed in disbelief— not because of how much money this event had brought in, but because once again, I knew I was not alone. There was a group of people on the other side working with me; I had a team, and I knew they had done this. Because I desired

to serve Spirit, and wanted to dedicate my life to this service, they found a way to

teach me, to pay for the classes I needed in order to serve them in the best way

possible.

Oh, and those events in LaPlata, how did they go? Well, they were

amazing! I was very nervous about doing this event, it was my biggest yet and this

was before I had hired an assistant, so I was checking people in, answering

questions, giving instructions on how it all worked, and conducting the event all

on my own. I had no time to pray or meditate, let alone to prepare, but thankfully

the readings were not affected, despite the many directions I was being pulled in

before I started. The evidence and messages rolled out of me faster and more

accurately than ever before. I had never experienced readings like this! I also

realized, after this event, why so many mediums talk about feeling "drained" after

reading people. Holy cow, I could hardly keep my eyes open on that drive home!

Aside from developing the confidence needed to do this work (and trust

me, at some point all mediums struggle with not having enough confidence) the

hardest part of becoming a public medium was learning to trust Spirit. We have to

trust not only that they are going to put us in the right places at the right times in

front of the right people, but also that they will give us the right evidence to provide proof to our sitters, that we are indeed connecting with their passed loved one. I don't know about you, but for a person that struggles with trust issues as it is, this was no easy task, however, through the years I have learned to trust them, and it's by far the best leap of faith I have ever taken.

I'll never forget the first guy that came through for me in LaPlata that day. It was a young man that had been involved in a fatal car accident; he had just become a father, not long before his passing. When he came through, he gave plenty of evidence that allowed me to anchor him to his girlfriend (the mother of his child), but he also gave me something that didn't make a bit of sense. He showed me the number 28, neither the girlfriend nor her mother could figure out what was so significant about that particular number.

I'll admit, it drives me crazy when I can't correctly interpret what Spirit is showing me for my sitters. It makes me feel like I am not serving Spirit to the best of my ability. Now, remember, this was very early in my career, and before any proper training, but still, I took blows like this hard. I had not yet grasped the concept that Spirit will never waste a thought, or that every single thing they show me always means something. Nor had I discovered how often my sitters would experience bouts of memory loss when they were put on the spot in front of a bunch of people to recall something that happened five years ago. Over the next few years messages and emails from former clients who had been given information that they claimed didn't make sense at the time of their reading, would prove that said information was in fact completely on target. Getting this feedback was a huge building block for my confidence. It took a while, but being told "No, that doesn't make sense" then, getting one of those nice lengthy emails after the event explaining that it did, helped me develop trust in Spirit even more, which, as I am sure you've gathered, is absolutely essential in this line of work.

On the way home from the LaPlata event I received a message via Facebook messenger from the woman who had lost the father of her baby in a wreck. She said when she returned to pick up her infant son, the babysitter told her that the child's shirt had gotten wet and they had to change him. When she looked at the shirt the child had been changed into, she noticed it: the huge number 28 on the front of his shirt.

A few months after the LaPlata event I would be on my way to York, Maine, to study Psychic Science, Mediumship, and Platform (also known as on stage) Mediumship with John Holland and the late Janet Nohavec (who was an accredited Arthur Findlay tutor—the real-life version of the Harry Potter Hogwarts school). I chose these mediums to study under not only because my intuition drew me to them, but because I appreciated their style of reading greatly. I felt their practical approach to the subjects were admirable and in depth and I loved the fact that Janet was a former Catholic nun. I would later also study forensic mediumship in New York under Lisa Williams. I cannot say enough good things about the classes and workshops these three individuals have brought to mankind.

Straight off the plane I rented a white Jeep and headed down the coast! I could literally taste the salt in the air, windows down and hair in the wind, headed toward my dream career, the very thing I had been running from for so long. This was the first time I had ever left my children overnight! Ledger, my son wasn't even two yet, but I knew I had to do this. I knew this training would give me the education I so desperately needed to fully step into my power.

I stayed at a place called The Stage Neck Inn, which was like a reset for my soul! Some of the things I picked up from these classes included: learning how to focus my mind and be aware of that focus, which also helped later in life with meditation in general; the differences between psychic information and mediumistic information; the structure of Spirit; as well as how to hold and maintain a link with Spirit for longer periods of time than I had formerly been able to. I also learned how to develop my own style of mediumship, in order to best represent each individual Spirit as the "person" they were. In addition, I picked up a term I use heavily today called, "mind-mapping," which is basically the mechanics and meanings behind signs and symbols within our mind. It is the very personal language that is created between the Spirit world and myself and is completely unique to each and every medium. Learning three-way communication techniques also helped greatly; as you can imagine, it is not easy to go from human communication to Spirit communication all in the same breath (imagine being in a conversation about the same topic with two other people who both speak a different language). Another skill I mastered while working with John and Janet was how to put myself into and bring myself out of an altered state at the drop of a hat, a skill that would prove imperative while in front of an audience.

Learning how to master existence as a spiritual being in a material world was probably the most surprising but useful skill I picked up while out east. Telepathy and remote viewing were already two of my strong suits and even those abilities were enhanced. In between classes I would take my shoes off and walk along the beach, which was so serene. There was also a cute little pub down the road from the Stage Neck Inn that I had dinner and drinks at, I can't remember the name, but it was delicious, and I really enjoyed people watching the locals! I made sure to visit an authentic light house while there as well, and that was my favorite part of the whole trip!

Eventually I would combine the skills I learned from these incredible souls, along with my own personal set of abilities, to create classes here in the Midwest. I was and still am very passionate about teaching metaphysics, mainly because there were no in person courses or mentors near my hometown when I discovered my life's purpose. It was a scary thing to navigate alone, so I wanted to offer a place that others could go to for questions and guidance once they too discovered their own abilities. To date, I have helped many flourishing psychics and mediums start their very own spiritual practice and I have to say, next to bringing comfort and healing to those hurting from a physical loss, there is no better feeling than knowing I was able to help someone else bring that same feeling to so many who desperately need it.

But first let me back things up a bit for you. Let's go on a little adventure shall we?

Chapter 2

The Early Years

It was December, I was about four years old, living in the tiny town of Philadelphia, Missouri (about 26 miles west of where I live now) in a tall, two-story white house. My mother and her sister Lana had gone for a well-deserved girls' night out, while my younger brother Keith and I were home with my grandmother.

I must have fallen asleep before she got home because I recall waking up in the middle of the night sandwiched between my her (my mom) and brother on the couch. I distinctly remember the beautiful warm glow from the lights on our Christmas tree filling the whole room; it felt so peaceful. I couldn't tell you what time it was—I remember very little because I was so young—but what I would wake up to next, would stay with me forever.

I was drifting in and out of sleep, struggling to get comfortable, when I looked up at the tree again. This time I saw a tall, dark man in a long, black coat and a black hat, standing in front of our Christmas tree. He was soaking wet, with water dripping from his hat and coat, and he was staring directly at me, right into my eyes. No words, no sounds, other than the crackling of the fire in our woodstove.

For a moment, I was frozen with fear. I reached over to my mother's leg and shook her awake; I said something to the effect of "Mommy, who's that man?" I could tell my words alarmed her by the way her voice sounded when she whispered, "What man?" into my ear. I said, "The tall man in the long black coat, he's all wet." She said, very calmly, "Don't move."

I closed my eyes, hoping this would make him disappear. It worked, and I quickly fell back asleep.

The next day, I remember waking up to a frantic conversation between my mother and Aunt Lana. Apparently the night before, on their way home, my mother and aunt had a crazy, unexplainable experience. As they were driving home, a black coat flew up onto the hood of the car, covering the windshield and blocking their view for just a split second. They pulled off to the side of the road, panic-stricken, assuming they must have just hit someone—but when they got out of the car, they saw nothing. No coat, no dent, not a single soul in sight.

After we moved out, the white house I saw the tall dark man in was demolished and made into a church parking lot. But to this day I still can't look at my own Christmas tree as an adult and not be creeped out—I have this fear that one Christmas, he's going to pop back in and scare the shit out of me!

I believe the spirit I saw that night had something to do with what my mother and aunt experienced on that cold winter night. I also believe that Spirit started placing these kinds of experiences into my life at a very young age to prepare me for what would lie ahead. Gently exposing me to bits and pieces of Spirit encounters, telepathy, and premonitions, so that when it was time for me to step up, I would have these encounters in my memory bank, to validate my newfound ability.

Always ready for the camera! Check out four-year-old Britney just hangin' out with my homeboy, Jesus.

Within a year, my five-year-old self would have another experience, just across the street, while staying the night with my Aunt Lana. She made my favorite thing for dinner that night, macaroni and tomatoes. This is still a favorite in our family and I strongly feel my aunt makes it the best (macaroni noodles, a can of tomato sauce, a ton of butter, salt and pepper, enjoy)!

I was putting my bowl in the sink, and when I turned around, to my surprise, there was lady in a colorful outfit just staring at me! It looked like she was pushing a cart of some kind, or maybe a baby stroller. I gasped and ran back into the living room to tell my aunt what I had just seen, in turn completely freaking her out for the rest of the night. After that, I don't recall having any similar experiences again until about age 12.

The year 2001 was the age of Harry Potter, Lord of the Rings, and (my favorite) the movie *Halloween Town* on Disney (that last one came out in 1998, but it was a big part of my childhood, so I had to throw it in there). By this time my mom had long since remarried and I had gained a new little brother! It was a great year to be a 12-year-old with an insatiable obsession for everything magical! I couldn't get enough—my attraction to the magical and mysterious was out of this world. I was mesmerized by shows like *Are You Afraid of the Dark, Bewitched,* and even *Unsolved Mysteries.*

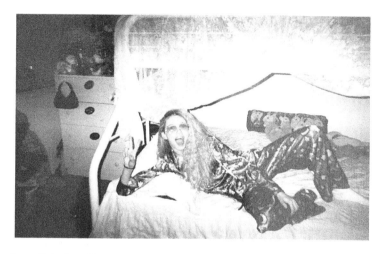

At age 12, I collected bunnies, everything magical, and I wanted to be a model when I grew up!

One night, while lying in bed, I was having trouble falling asleep—not uncommon for me, as I have struggled with insomnia my entire life. I remember looking into my vanity mirror; within it, I could see the doorway into my room. I began to see what I thought was a shadow move in and out of the doorway— almost as if someone was playing peek-a-boo with me.

Once again, I was frozen with fear, but I noticed something about the hairline of the shadow figure bobbing in and out of my door frame: it looked exactly like that of my mother's sister, who had passed at age 18, long before I was born. Aunt Gail had very distinct, wavy hair that went down her back. I remember feeling absolutely certain in that moment that this was her—which was bizarre to me. How could I be absolutely sure about something, with no proof at all?!

Nevertheless, family member or not I was still petrified, and after several minutes found the courage to scream for my mother. I don't know what I was more afraid of at that time: the spirit in my doorway or waking up my father for something I was sure he would think I was lying about. Either way, I did it—I screamed like a banshee!

My mother came in immediately, flipped on the hallway light, and rushed to my bedside. I told her what I had seen, and she said, "I have seen it too, it's okay, she's just checking on you." Which was comforting, but I was still totally freaked out.

After that, I would see what I call "shadow people" several more times. It was a frightening experience for me, because I knew what I saw would be hard to describe and I also felt that if I told other people they would think I was full of shit. I didn't feel like these shadow people were there to harm me, but I also didn't understand the point of me seeing them if I couldn't communicate with them or even see their faces. Despite having this same encounter many more times, I would not disclose said encounters to anyone else again until adulthood.

Just before my 13th birthday, I began having a very strange but simple dream. I saw these really old, worn-out, feminine-looking, fabric-like black boots on someone's feet. The feet and legs looked like they were slowly spinning around and around in a circle. It was like I was looking down at these boots from above, and that was it. That was the dream. Strange, right? I'll elaborate more on this later, but I wanted to make sure I mentioned it at the time in which it occurred in my life.

I was really into history as a child. I loved watching history TV shows and enjoyed reading about how people hundreds of years ago lived their lives: what they ate, what they did for entertainment, what they wore. I remember going into an antique store with my mother once and seeing this beautiful ivory and tan vintage dress. It was pretty expensive, but when I ran my fingers across the fabric, I knew I had to have it. At the time I did not recognize what I was feeling exactly; however, now I feel that on some level my soul recognized this style of clothing or perhaps even this exact dress itself.

I begged my mother for this gown, and even though she probably couldn't afford it at the time, she bought it for me anyway (thanks again, mom). It fit like a glove, like it was made for me. I would spend hours on end wearing it, just sitting in its history. I loved how it made feel and the visions that came with it. I would eventually do a photo shoot in that dress a couple years later at age 15.

The mysterious white and tan antique dress that stole hours of my childhood.

Speaking of history, social studies class with Mr. Stout was one of my favorite classes of all time, but there was one subject in particular that was about to blow my mind. Yep: the Salem Witch Trials of 1692, in Salem, Massachusetts.

We were instructed to open our textbooks to a particular page and Mr. Stout began his lecture. He explained that during the Salem Witch Trials, a series of hearings and prosecutions were conducted, during which individuals were charged with witchcraft, based on suspicious behavior and/or hearsay from other colony members. Between 1692 and 1693 more than two hundred people were accused of witchcraft, 30 people were found guilty,18 were executed by hanging, and one poor gentleman was pressed to death, in an effort to get an admission of guilt—for a total of 19 senseless executions.

While listening to my teacher explain the details of one of America's darkest moments in history, I began to feel some sort of way. I became very emotional, and I felt a heaviness in my chest I couldn't ignore. I felt very connected to what happened to these people, it was like they were my own family or something! This overwhelming feeling of empathy was not new to me; what was new, was feeling this way about people I had no real physical connection too. I wouldn't understand what I had experienced in that classroom until many years later.

I was thirsty for more information on the Salem Witch Trials. I wanted details: first and last names, family histories, exact reasons why these people were accused in the first place, and most importantly, what happened after it was all said and done. Did magistrate John Hathorne ever realize the slaying of these innocent people was all just one big mistake?

After school that day I walked eight blocks from my house to the Marion County library at the center of our small town, and wouldn't you know it, they had just one book on the subject. I checked it out, took it home, and soaked up every single word. I looked at that book every single day and night for a week straight, reading and rereading the same pages over and over again just to see if I missed anything, running my fingers over the pictures of what Salem looks like today, and imagining what it must be like to live there. Then I walked back to the library and checked it out again, and again, and again. Something about that book made me feel like I had a place, or a connection to something bigger, something important; it made me feel like I knew something about myself, at an age and time in my life when nothing else made sense (hello awkwardness, hello puberty).

By age 13, my desire to "fit in" and be normal would take over, but for some that's easier said than done. Especially when I was so unbelievably aware of my conscience—you know that little voice within in you that tells you "don't do it" but you do it anyways? Yeah, mine sounds like a fucking foghorn.

Other girls my age were sneaking over to older boys' houses, drinking alcohol, smoking, making out, and doing all the stuff most parents would ground you for. When I tried to fit in with them, it felt hollow, icky, and meaningless. I was awkward, super skinny, and I asked way too many questions. I didn't lie to my parents (well, not often, I'm sure I did at some point) and I was constantly concerned about the consequences of my actions.

It was always a struggle for me to take an interest in the silly trends my female classmates were going wild over: the hottest brand-named clothing, ridiculous movies, or the latest pop or rap songs that repeated the same annoying words over and over again until it drove you insane. I was not an outcast by any means—I had a few close friends—but I most definitely wasn't doing the things that needed to be done for me to fit in with the popular girls either, and that made those early teen years even harder for me. I would tell myself many times a day, "None of this matters, none of this will matter in the future, you just have to get through school, and everything will get better, everything will make more sense once you're older." I didn't realize how insightful these thoughts were at such a young age until my editor mentioned it, but looking back, I too am surprised at my mindset as a teenager.

Over time I came to realize that trying to fit in was too much work, and simply not worth the end result. I had nothing in common with these people. I craved heavy metal and rock and roll music, I wore expressive clothing instead of being concerned with brand names like Hollister and American Eagle, and I threw myself into books and mysteries, while focusing on the few but genuine friends I

had in my life.

I was the most well-behaved 14-year-old rebel. I hated school with a passion, but this drama class
was fun!

Just before my fourteenth birthday, I took a serious interest in modeling. I

signed a modeling contract with an agency out of St. Louis, Missouri, and rather

quickly began making a name for myself as a teenage model—nothing

inappropriate, always fully clothed, as I was still very much a child. I was

extremely passionate about modeling; it was around this same time that also

started competing in local and state pageants.

Clearly, modeling isn't an acceptable talent for pageants, so I began taking private clogging lessons, something my mother was very spirited about. Had I known then what I know now: talking to dead people would have been a way cooler talent! I can only imagine what the judges' and pageant directors' faces would have looked like.

My parents were incredibly supportive and for the first time in my life I felt normal. I was making goals, I had attainable aspirations for my future, and it felt good. I finally felt like I had a focus and direction in life, which I not only enjoyed and was good at, but most importantly made my parents proud. It was a relief; it had been so hard watching my classmates excel in extracurricular activities like sports or choir. Up until that point I remember feeling like I was just existing, like there was nothing special about me, like I was letting them down, but after I found these two hobbies, for the first time in my life I finally felt like I fit in somewhere. I thought to myself, *after 14 years, I have finally given my parents something to brag about*. That's all I ever really wanted to do, make my parents proud of me.

Sadly, even after finding something I felt I was good at, no matter how much I ate I couldn't gain weight. This lead to me being ridiculed almost daily for being "too skinny," by older family members and class mates, which in turn resulted in me becoming increasingly self-conscious and developing a crippling level of anxiety.

At 16 I would land a full fashion spread in *Alive* magazine.

Seeking
Enlightenment
find harmony
this season in
boho whites
& hippy chic
brights

Photography by
Rick Gould

Hair & Makeup
by Theresa Miller

Interestingly enough, having no prior knowledge of what I would eventually be doing as a psychic medium, the upper right photo was taken of me in a meditative pose and the spread titled "Seeking Enlightenment."

Riding the Miss Missouri Outstanding Teen Float for a parade in Mexico, Missouri. Black dress and flowers after winning Jr. Miss Northeast Missouri. And below, posing for Miss Teen Hannibal.

By the time I had taken on my favorite title, Miss Teen Hannibal, I was 16. Becoming an ambassador to this community was not a responsibility I took lightly, and so, I left my metaphysical obsessions and rebellious desires in the dust. I assumed that I was just growing out of that phase of my life and becoming a young adult, I accepted it and stepped into my new role confidently. Life was good, it was exciting, it was full of possibilities.

Chapter 3

The Secret

Apparently 2007 was a big year for anyone that spelled their name B.R.I.T.N.E.Y. I didn't lose my shit or shave my head, (if you recall, the Britney Spears fiasco) but the summer after my high school graduation I did have a life-changing experience that would stay with me for the rest of my life, something that I would unknowingly allow to influence me for many years to come. I was so excited about my future after graduation!

Over the last five years, I had developed a level of confidence that allowed me to walk onto a stage and perform without fear. I have always had a keen sense of what to do next, which probably has something to do with the high levels of intuition coursing through my body—that or I was just another cocky teenager. I guess what I am trying to say here is, I trusted myself—or at least I did, before *this* happened.

The summer following my high school graduation, I took a waitressing job as a Hooter's girl in Columbia, Missouri, with the intent to enroll at The University of Missouri, also known as Mizzou, that fall. I was so fucking excited about the freedom that was going to come with being a young adult; I could not wait to get out of my tiny town and experience life. I was looking forward to new friendships, adult experiences, and most of all to finding my purpose in life, whatever that may be.

Columbia is about two hours south of my hometown (Palmyra, Missouri). I was still competing in pageants and actively modeling, but I wanted to be a part of something deeper, something more challenging. I didn't feel like I was making a big enough impact; modeling did not fulfill me on its own, it was more therapeutic than anything. I felt a career in modeling would not keep the lights on, at least not in Missouri, so I decided to study psychology, as I have always been fascinated with how the human mind works.

Hooters was never in my plan of things to do after graduation. I just happened to be eating at a Hooters while visiting some friends in Columbia when I was offered a job. I had no place to live until the fall, or money to get a place of my own for that matter. I remember the hiring manager eagerly telling me not to worry about that issue. He said, "We will find you a place to live until you can afford rent, you just focus on getting yourself down here."

The following week, I packed up all of my belongings and I headed to Columbia. My car was out of commission, so my dad arranged for me to borrow my grandfather's little tan S10 pickup, until my car was fixed.

Hooters was my first stop! There were a few tests I needed to take before it was official, including things like proper etiquette, uniform and picture rules, hygiene expectations, and of course WINGS—I had to know everything about the wings!

After my tests the manager introduced me to Mandy. She had offered me her couch until school started. She was shorter than I was, with long, thick dark-blond hair and beautiful big brown eyes. She was sweet, and she had an innocence about her that instantly put me at ease. I remember thinking, *if this girl can make it here, I'll be just fine!*

We went to the back of the restaurant, where there was a dressing room for the girls to get ready in before each shift. There was a mirror that had big fancy light bulbs all around it complete with a counter to do your make up at, as well as lockers, and even a vending machine that had extra pairs of socks and panty hose for purchase should you need a new pair. They gave me a size extra small in their famous neon-orange silky shorts and tank top, along with a brown apron, shiny nude tights, a fancy name tag, and my favorite, the big '80s-style slouchy white socks. I still wear those socks to this day!

The Hooters girls were like one big family, it was a total blast to work there! The managers at the Columbia establishment took great care of all their girls. They were protective, they always walked us to our cars after a late-night shift, and most importantly they stood up to inappropriate diners on our behalf .

One night, the girls were talking about going out for drinks after work. I asked them how they planned to get into clubs, as most of us were under 21 at the time. Sarah (who went on to win Miss. Hooters International) flashed a quick smile at me, then whipped out her fake ID. I instantly grabbed it to take a closer look—at first glance it did look just like her! Guess who else it looked like? Yep, yours truly! She said, "You can use it anytime you want!"

I became giddy with excitement about the idea of being able to just walk into a club or bar and experience uncharted territory—I wanted to see what all the fuss was about!

A couple days later, that time came. Mandy got into a huge fight with her boyfriend Michael and decided she wanted to have a few drinks to let off some steam, she asked if I wanted to tag along. I said "Sure!" I was totally up for it.

This small-town girl knew nothing about going to a club, or even a bar for that matter, I had no idea what to expect. I went to the mall and picked out a super cute outfit, then stopped by Hooters to grab the fake ID from Sarah. It was late, but most people didn't go out until after 10 p.m. there, which was a shocking concept to me!

While I was waiting for Mandy to get back to our apartment (she had left to talk things over with Michael) she sent a text that said, "Hey I don't think I should go out, I know it will make things way worse and he will be really mad at me if I go. I'm sorry girl."

I stood there at the front door contemplating what I should do. I remember hearing "don't go" but I assumed it was just my good girl conscience creeping in as usual. I know now that my intuition, angels, and guides were working overtime to keep this night from happening, but, like any teenager fresh out of high school, I didn't listen. I was so pumped—this was exactly why I had left home, so I could have new experiences like this, right? I let that excitement and lust for new adventures override my intuition.

I arrived at the club, fake ID in hand. I could hear the loud music from the club from inside my truck as I pulled up. As I got out, again I heard it, "don't go in." Assuming it was just my nerves, because I was about to try to pull one over on this giant-ass bouncer, I went ahead and got in line anyway.

This dude looked like he *lived* to call out fake IDs. The line was getting shorter and shorter. When it was finally my turn, I handed him the ID (while repeating in my head, *just be cool, don't be obvious, act normal*). He paused for what seemed like a century, he looked at me then looked back at the ID, he did this several times. I smiled at him, probably looking every bit as guilty as the kid he had thrown out right ahead of me, but to my surprise and in a voice that basically said, *I'm not stupid, but tonight is your lucky night,* he said "Go on." In typical teenage Britney fashion, I jumped up and down like I had won the goddamn lottery and thanked him with a hug. *Way to be cool, Britney, way to be cool.*

I made my way up to the bar; I assumed after buying that new outfit I probably had just enough money for two drinks max. I ordered what the girl ahead of me did, a cranberry and vodka, and then headed to the back. This place was dimly lit, it was really pretty dark; it was equal parts shiny-metal and wood finish, both retro and rustic. The feeling in the club was depressing and lonely to me, not at all what I expected, though the place was packed. I told myself, *maybe it just feels this way because you don't know a single soul in this place.*

Doing my best to hide how awkward I felt, I spotted a huge window. It looked like there was a wraparound deck attached to the club, because I could see people on the other side of it. I headed straight for the back door—ahh, fresh air! I walked over to the cedar banister and looked out at this body of water behind the club. It was really beautiful.

I finished my drink and debated whether I should even get another or just go back to Mandy's. Just as I was about to go back inside and leave the club disappointed, this super-cute and clearly intoxicated guy walked up to me. He said, "Hi, I'm Ben, my friends said I didn't have the balls to come ask you for your number and normally I wouldn't but tonight I have liquid courage, so what do ya say, can I get your number?"

I laughed and paused for a moment, then he said, "You can just write something fake on this napkin, you don't really have to give it to me." I smiled really big at him, and said, "Sure, I'll give you my number." He said, "YES!! This is awesome, so is this really your number or is this a fake?" I smiled again, and said, "No, this is really my number."

I remember thinking how cute it was watching him struggle to quickly get his hand in and out of his pocket to retrieve a crumpled-up, slightly wet receipt. He then proceeded to write his own number on it and gave it to me, saying,

"Here, this is mine, in case I lose yours and you don't hear from me." He was very sweet.

He asked if I wanted to join him and his friends at their table, so I peeked around him to get a better look at his group. Nearly every one of them had their eyes on us, but it looked like a decent group of people and there were several girls with them, so I said, "Let me go get another drink and I'll be right back."

I walked up to the bar and ordered another cranberry and vodka. I waited at the bar for what seemed like forever. The first drink had come super quick, and he made it right there in front of me. I recall thinking, *why did he go to the other side of the bar, maybe he ran out of juice or something?*

After about ten minutes this thin, intelligent-looking man with brown hair brushing past his eyes handed me my drink. I sipped on it as I walked back outside to join Ben and his friends on the deck.

After just a few sips, I began to feel what I can only describe as intense vertigo. I thought that the drink was just stronger this time, that or the liquor must have finally caught up with me; after all, I was a complete lightweight. I assumed I was just really drunk.

I sat down, and just as I did the lights got bright and they announced last call. Ben grabbed my hand and said, "Hey, do you need a ride?" I tried to stand up to follow his group out, but I felt like I had forgotten how to use my arms and legs.

Out of nowhere, this guy walked up to us, just as Ben was offering me a ride, and said, "Hey, I can take her home, we live right across from each other." I looked up and was surprised to see, my neighbor, he lived like right next to Mandy's place. It was a weird set up but essentially we shared a split duplex within a giant apartment complex. Our front doors faced each other. I was surprised he even recognized me—I had only seen this guy like twice, walking from his car to his door, that's it.

I looked back at Ben and made what would be the worst decision of my life. I didn't know this Ben dude, honestly I didn't know the neighbor guy either—but for me, neighbor, was better than a complete stranger. I didn't want to get in a car with a potential psychopath, going who knows where.

Neighbor guy had dark, almost black, stick-straight hair, long and untamed; I remember him tucking it back behind his ear and seeing his pronounced sideburns. He and a buddy of his were on either side of me, helping me walk to their large black Escalade. *Why are these guys being so nice to me?* A feeling of dread came over me, I'll never forget that vehicle; there was a third man, he was the driver. He pulled right up to us and they helped me in the back. As soon as I sat down I passed out.

The next thing I remember is being slumped over someone's shoulders, upside down, being carried up a flight of carpeted stairs. I felt pressure in my head as the blood flowed straight to it. I lifted my head up for just a moment to see what was happening, and I came face to face with a man that was walking behind the man who was carrying me. A huge smile formed across his face and he said, "She's waaaaaking uuuuupp" but it didn't last long, I passed out again.

The next thing I would wake up to would haunt me for the rest of my life. They noticed that I was waking up again and I'm sure they saw the look of panic on my face. I tried to move my arms and push them away, but my arms would not do what I told them to do. I tried to kick them, but my legs wouldn't move. One of them whispered, "Hey, hey, it's okay, we're taking care of you, we got you." I guess this was his lame attempt to try to console me, that or this fuckwad had no conscience and was just a sick son of a bitch. I opened my mouth, and to this day I'm not sure what came out. I know that my intention was to scream but whatever I did didn't hinder them; in fact, they just laughed. That's all I remember from that night.

I woke up at eight a.m. the next day, I know because there was an alarm clock on the floor next to this piss-poor excuse for a bed I was on. No sheets or covers, and one shitty stained pillow. They had attempted to put my clothes back on, but I could tell I didn't dress myself; and the bralette I was wearing was missing.

I sat up on the bed. It felt like I had been hit by a truck, my head was pounding. I looked around the room for my shoes and purse but couldn't find either; I was alone in the room. I slowly started to replay what little I could remember in my head. When I realized what happened I began to panic. *Who is on the other side of that door? Did I ask for this? Do they know that I know what they did to me? Why did they just let me sleep here? Isn't an actual rape supposed to end with me dead in a ditch or something? What in the actual fuck!?*

I opened the door. I could hear a TV was on but saw no one. I started to walk down the stairs, shoeless—at this point I just wanted to get the heck out of there, I'd figure out the rest once I was out of this hellhole.

Just as I hit the last step this short shaggy-looking guy came around the corner holding a video game controller. I instantly recognized him as one of the three, he was the driver. He smiled and said "Hey, so last night was fun," running his fingers through his hair. It was like that one meaningless gesture, that one line, was his way of telling me he was sorry.

He spoke again: "Hey, um, bathroom's open if you want to take a shower or something?" At the time it didn't register why he wanted me to take a shower.

I was still frozen at this point, humiliated, looking at him like a deer in headlights. I said, "Oh, um, no thanks, I think I'm just going to take one when I get home, ya know, I'm like, right there," pointing to the door as I literally lived ten steps away. I saw my purse was on the counter and went to grab it.

He then gave me a look that scared the living fuck out of me. My mind instantly went into fight or flight mode. The look on his face told me he was serious, and I recall in that moment thinking, *oh, he remembers me waking up a during the assault*. The last thing I wanted was for him to kill my ass, because he was scared I would turn him in to the police or something.

I walked into the bathroom. He turned on the water and walked out. I thought, *how does he even know I'm getting in?* I remember thinking how sick and twisted it was that this son of a bitch was trying to play this off like it was just your normal one-night stand, or like, some kind of casual after club hook up—it really pissed me off. Everything in me wanted to scream at him, confront him, put him in his goddamn place! I wanted to say, "I know what you fucking did" but I was scared, and still really confused. I was ashamed and embarrassed that these men had just seen me in such a way. I was mortified, I felt like every bit of pride I had, was stripped away from me that night.

Instead, I turned the water up as hot as I could stand it and stood there under the water, thinking about the night before. I tried to replay everything that had happened within the last 24 hours in my mind. I remembered working from ten a.m. to four p.m.; I made great tips that day. I made plans with Mandy after she got into that fight with her boyfriend. I left the apartment to go pick out something cute to wear and get that fake ID. I came back and got ready, just before it was time to leave, she canceled on me—then boom, it hit me.

I was warned. I completely disregarded my intuition, I ignored my gut instincts, but even worse, I did something that was entirely illegal! I can't go to the police, they might arrest me for using a fake ID, then that would get Sarah and her sister in trouble and I will be known as a snitch, and no one will ever want to hang out with me again. Oh my God, I could be arrested for drinking underage too!

I can't tell my parents; they would be so disappointed in me. They would assume I wasn't responsible enough to handle life as an adult if they knew what happened. Plus, ewe, gross, I don't want them to know that happened to me. I honestly felt like there was nothing I could do and no where I could go. I told myself, *you deserved this, this is what happens when you don't follow the rules. Stupid girl, stupid, stupid, stupid!*

Ok, this is weird, and I don't know why, but as a kid and teenager I always worried about being sexually assaulted—maybe it was a past-life thing, or maybe it was completely normal, and all girls fear this. Either way, there was a point before moving to Columbia where I thought to myself, *I made it, nobody touched me.* I realize that's a fucked-up and morbid notion, but I thought it—then this happened. *Stupid girl, you brought this on yourself, with your short, tight dress, your high heels, your blonde hair and makeup, you wanted to be noticed! This is what you get, this is your own fault!*

By that time, I assumed I had been in there long enough. I got out and grabbed the towel he left for me on the sink and quickly dried off; it smelled like mildew. I was still wet on my legs and back but all I wanted to do was get my clothes on and get the hell out of there.

When I walked out, the guy was sitting with another man that I had never seen before. He looked up at me and said, "You alright?" the concern in his voice was laughable. I said "Yeah," and he said, "Okay, have a good one."

That was it—I walked out of that nightmare. When I opened their door and could see my apartment door, I felt such a sense of relief, I could breathe again.

I walked in and sat down on the couch—thank God, no one was there. I curled up in a ball and cried. I cried because I was alone, far from home, and totally ashamed. So, this is what it feels like to be violated.

The significance of what those men did to me wouldn't set in for years. I don't know if I just blocked it out because I was mortified and disgusted with myself, or if I was worried that if I told people they wouldn't believe me, or worse, some might think I brought it on myself by being in a place I shouldn't have. Either way, I felt I couldn't tell anyone about this.

After about an hour of sulking, I packed up all of my belongings, loaded them up in my grandpa's truck, stopped by Hooters, quit my job, left Sarah her ID in the Hooters dressing room, and drove straight home. In my mind, home was the only thing that could take away this lonely, icky feeling. I just wanted to be back home, where it was safe.

I had just signed a year lease on a new apartment that I was supposed to move into in a month, once I started college. I had to beg the owner of the apartment building to not charge me every month for the next year for the cost of that place. I begged him to let me find someone to take over my lease, I was not going back there! Thankfully, he gave in, and let me out of the damn thing. I

moved on, I put this whole thing in my rearview mirror, and I picked up my life

where I had left off before moving away. My father wasn't disappointed—more

confused, than anything, but that was a relief to me. I wouldn't tell him or my

mother about what happened until about 12 years later, during the process of

writing this book.

I have worked through the emotional effects of this experience in several

different ways, and I will discuss more on that towards the end of this book. I

would also meet friends over the next decade who'd had similar things happen to

them. I felt like I was safe talking about it with them, because they understood

how I felt and why I didn't tell anyone, that was therapeutic in itself—but up until

the publication of this book only about five people knew what happened to me

that summer.

When the Me-Too movement hit social media, it changed my views on

becoming public with my story. Not because I wanted to jump on the

bandwagon—quite the opposite actually. It made my blood boil to see how so

many men (and even some women) ridiculed the movement and the brave

women that shared their stories, lumping those women into the same category as

others who'd made false accusations of sexual assault with their thoughtless posts on social media. Every day for months I'd see men (some I actually loved and cared deeply for) post about the fear they had for themselves and their sons, as if the majority of rape accusations were false. I'd see memes that made fun of people that were strong enough to share that they were assaulted with the public, and it infuriated me. The fact that so many men mocked women for being a part of this movement sent me into a fury, these woman were sharing raw, painful, stories in order to bring awareness to the fact that sexual assault happens more often than you think, in an effort to make others who kept it a secret (like myself) feel less alone. These dick heads and their actions are the very reason so many women suffer in silence and never tell anyone. Through this I started to notice how society still to this day prioritizes the male point of view over that of women. The Me-Too movement turned me into a straight fucking feminist and opened my eyes as to why the world needs more women willing to stand up to slime ball men (and in some cases, slime ball women). It made me realize why I'd kept it a secret all this time to begin with and it also made me understand why it's so unbelievably important to go to the police, get a rape kit done, and turn these pieces of shit in. By doing so you are essentially saving the next girl or guy. It proved to me that what I did in the wake of that horror was exactly why they do what they do. I kept my mouth shut, hung my head in shame, even considered that I may have played some kind of role in this happening to me, and saddest of all, I feared that no one would believe me.

Not one single time did I post "me too" or publicly comment about my own personal experience—but I wanted to, I wanted to so damn bad. I wanted to lash out at every one of those assholes, but I didn't.

I don't believe social media outlets are a place to unload something this big and I was not about to put this out there and have it minimalized in any way, and frankly I wasn't ready.

Not long after this happened, I met Andrew Buckwalter, a tattooist at a local shop here in Hannibal. After giving me my first tattoo, he offered me a job as his secretary, and we began dating about five months into my working there. He was ten years older than me; I was only 19 at the time, because of that I felt tremendous pressure to act mature as possible. My main goal, after we started dating, was to find a "good, stable job." My mother was a dental assistant, so I knew something of the trade. After landing my first job as a dental assistant, we settled into life as a working couple and I assumed this was what I was supposed to be doing as an "adult": waking up, going to work, paying bills, and living for weekend adventure with my boyfriend. This went on for a couple of years and we eventually got married.

Chapter 4

Make Them Proud

By 24 I had tried every type of job you can imagine. I had worked everywhere from a Hooters to a Country Club as a waitress; one time I almost got hit by a semi-truck while waitressing at a Cassano's when it crashed into the building and hit the table I was waiting on (everyone was ok, but I peed myself and I quit the next day). I worked at the YMCA; the bank; the radio station, the gas station, the Hannibal visitors center, and tried retail too. I was once an aide for an elementary school, where I quickly realized my mouth did not belong; I was a secretary at a tattoo shop (which as you know led to marriage); a vet tech; and even, wait for it, a Pure Romance consultant. That last one made it a little easier to come out as a medium—imagine telling your family you want to sling dildos on the side to get you through college, it was awkward, but I made bank.

I guess you could say I was vehement about finding my spot in the world. I never left a job without having the next one lined up. I was curious, and willing to try anything in hopes of finally finding something I was passionate about and enjoyed doing, but the truth of the matter was, none of those jobs did it for me. It was a struggle to walk into work each day, and not because it was work (I understand no one likes going to work) but because it felt like a huge-ass waste of time, I knew there was something better out there for me, but I just couldn't put my finger on it. I remember thinking, *it shouldn't feel like this, something is missing.*

For years I told myself to get over it and just do your job, no one loves their job, this is what being an adult is all about. After all, that's what I saw and heard growing up, but I was always on the lookout for something that I felt would better suit me.

After I got married, I decided to go to cosmetology school. I enrolled at a local school in Hannibal and felt really good about my decision—until I had to sign the financial papers asking to borrow eighteen thousand dollars. That was a scary moment! I pushed on, did my eleven months of training, and graduated. I had dreams of owning my own salon one day.

Late one night, not long after graduating from cosmetology school, I would have my first real psychic vision (or what some might call a premonition). To this day I laugh about this story every time I tell it, because it's just so random and silly, but it's a part of my story, so here goes.

I was lying in bed trying to fall asleep. My husband was in the living room playing a video game, while all I could think about was this Chinese food I'd had in a St. Louis mall about a month earlier, from a place called Panda Express. I was craving it so bad, I got up walked into the living room and said, "Andrew, I want Panda Express."

He laughed, and without looking away from the TV he said, "Well, that's a hell of a drive." The nearest Panda Express was about two hours away from us. I turned around and headed back to bed, but the second I laid down I had what I can only describe as a vision.

I saw a brand-new Panda Express built on the far end of the parking lot of a ShopKo, about 20 miles away in the next city over of Quincy, Illinois. I thought it was crazy, but on a whim, and in my mind totally joking, I walked back into the living room and confidently told Andrew what I had seen. I said, "You watch, it's gonna happen!"

A few weeks later, we were driving on Broadway in Quincy and as we approached the ShopKo ahead, I could see a big sign at the edge of their parking lot. As we got closer I saw that the sign read FUTURE HOME OF PANDA EXPRESS.

I literally stopped breathing for a second, I thought Andrew was going to run off the road. We both started laughing hysterically, but inside I knew this meant something—there was no way in hell you could just pull those specifics out of your ass! I was in disbelief: that "vision" had come true.

I remember being in an almost zombie-like state for the next couple of days, but I had no idea where to go, what to do, or who to ask about this sort of thing, so I went on with my life, and put it in the back of my mind. I had much bigger, more realistic interests and goals at that time anyway, like making a baby and my new cosmetology career!

I'd just graduated from cosmetology school and made plans to rent a booth from a local salon, Andrew and I had just moved into our first "nice" place, and we were working on that baby thing! Getting pregnant was something we'd been struggling with for a couple years at this point. Andrew being 35, and myself 25, it was really starting to get to me that we hadn't conceived yet, but I didn't let it bother me too much. I stayed focused at my new job at "The Strand" and was confident that I had finally found my niche in life.

On a beautiful October day, a girl named Corrie came into the salon. I had met her a few times before, through mutual friends while downtown having drinks—but I didn't know much about her, aside from the fact that I thought she was super sweet. She wanted a fresh fall cut and color.

I showed her to my chair and as she sat down she said, "So are you ready for Halloween!?" With excitement I said, "Oh yes, it's my favorite time of year!"— and in that very moment something familiar hit me like a ton of bricks. It was like my obsession with all things magical from my childhood came flooding back in.

While putting foils in her hair I began to tell her about something that I hadn't thought about or even talked about in nearly a decade. I shared with her my intense interests in Salem as a preteen, I told her about the boots dream, and about how I 've always longed to visit Salem. It felt so good to talk about this stuff, it felt different than when I was a kid, it was rejuvenating, maybe because now I was an adult?

She looked at me in the mirror and said, "You should go see my mom, she owns The Opened Book, I bet she would have some stuff you would be interested in." I said, "The Opened Book? What is that, like a bookstore?" She said, "Yes, but she's got other stuff too, like tarot cards, stones, and books on everything metaphysical!"

I thought, *wait a minute, how did I not know this place existed?* I'd been living in Hannibal for nearly six years and had never even heard of it!

Immediately after finishing Corrie's hair, I hopped into my Jeep and made the four-block drive down Mark Twain Avenue. *ohhh, there it is, ok I always wondered what this place was!*

I parked and walked up the little concrete steps that were surrounded by beautiful, blooming greenery on either side. It felt so magical, upon entering, I noticed a broom on the front door, as well as the sound of bells as I let myself in.

I was instantly greeted by the smell of incense, sage, homemade soaps, and old books. Before me sat a beautiful woman, with long gray hair and glasses… she was sitting on a giant exercise ball in front of her computer. She was situated behind a glass counter full of handmade jewelry, stones, tarot cards, and other treasures. She said, "Hello, can I help you find something?"

We talked for nearly an hour; I told her about my interests in the Salem Witch Trials, and how I'd always felt drawn to the mystical side of things. There was no judgment, she was so kind and understanding, and so full of wisdom. I could have stayed there all day, just soaking up every word out of her mouth.

After looking around for a while I told her I was interested in buying a deck of tarot cards. I had bought one about five years earlier but had no real idea of how to read them or what exactly to do with them. She suggested a beginner's deck that came with a how-to-read tarot book. When I walked out of that shop it felt like a ton of bricks had been lifted off of my chest, I felt refreshed, I could feel a positive shift in my energy. I rushed home and devoured that tarot book.

Not long after that, I started reading for myself and close friends. I was stunned at the accuracy of the readings, and I loved how natural it felt; it was the one thing in my life that felt completely effortless, which was the most fulfilling feeling I'd ever experienced.

However, this was not something I advertised, or even spoke about. I knew how deeply religious my husband's parents were and I worried about upsetting them with my new hobby—although to my parents, this type of news would have come as no surprise.

I also worried about how this new interest of mine would affect others close to me—would it change how they viewed me? Would they still respect me and take me seriously, or would they think I'd become a fuckin nutcase? This kind of behavior (worrying about what others think about me) still to this day baffles my friends and family, as I have never been one to worry about what others thought about me. Something felt different about this fear though; it felt deeply rooted inside of me, and soon I would understand exactly why.

About six months after my visit to The Opened Book, we got the news we had been hoping for: we were approved for IVF! I wanted nothing more than to have a baby, and after several tests had determined there was no physical reason as to why we had not yet conceived, we got the go-ahead from our doctor to give IVF a try.

I was over the moon. I made the appointment to visit the IVF clinic that our doctor recommended immediately. Of course, we had to wait a couple of weeks before seeing the specialists that make the baby magic happen, but I was just thrilled to be one step closer!

About a week later, while folding laundry, I found myself thinking about the appointment, when out of nowhere I heard a voice in my head say, "Don't do it." I was like, *What in the hell? That's strange—don't do it? What do you mean don't do it?*

It was louder and more audible than the voice I heard before going to the club. I was so confused, I even walked throughout the entire house, just to make absolutely sure there wasn't anyone in there with me!

Days went by and those words turned into a feeling that got stronger and stronger. I felt like someone was telling me to give up on my dream of having a family, and I was kind of pissed about it. I ended up canceling the appointment, although I was still feeling confused about why I was supposed to do that.

I decided to shift my focus from starting a family to opening up my own salon. I was so sick of hearing about how I was trying too hard or being told I just had to forget about it, then it would happen. I was sick of feeling depressed every time a pregnancy test came back negative I was sick of being frustrated every time I had to hear about someone we knew announcing their pregnancy. I was over this roller coaster that always seemed to end with me emotionally raw, and physically drained.

I found a nice little place to rent, just blocks from the historic downtown Hannibal area and riverfront. I basically decided that if we were meant to have children we would, and from this point forward I was going to embrace this new future in my head: a future that included a new business, more traveling, and less sadness and stress!

I don't know what exactly came over me, but I was no longer depressed about not doing IVF (and a little relieved, considering it was going to cost thousands and a baby was not even a guarantee). I was excited about a new adventure, and so The Beauty Bar was born! A classy salon that offered a free drink with every salon service!

Chapter 5

The Beauty Bar

The salon building needed some work. Not a lot, but some. It needed new flooring, some fresh paint, and some seriously new lighting. Chandeliers were a must! The rent for the building was extremely affordable, so I felt these updates were justified.

I found a dark-purple marble-looking floor tile on sale at Lowe's, purple and gold paint for the walls, and my dad offered to pay an electrician to strip out all the old ugly florescent lighting so I could have my chandeliers installed (thanks, again Dad). I ordered salon chairs, mirrors, and roll carts for each booth (four total), and of course we had a bar complete with bar stools! Everything was coming along wonderfully, until...

Just eight days into painting and laying the new floor, I started feeling weird, almost like my body was being invaded by a virus. Overnight, I felt like I had developed some kind of spidey senses; I was smelling things that others couldn't, feeling super-nauseous, and getting very emotional over the smallest things. It didn't dawn on me until the next day, after experiencing these strange symptoms for a full 24 hours, what it could be—and I thought to myself, *No way, no fucking way!*

On the morning of August 8th, 2013, at 6am I woke up and took a pregnancy test. It was positive.

I nearly fell off the toilet, I truly did. Andrew was still fast asleep upstairs, so I quietly I put on some pants and drove as fast as I could to Walmart. I bought seven tests. Every damn kind they had. I went into the Walmart bathroom and took them all (eww, I know, but I couldn't wait). I had to know for sure—and wouldn't you know it? All of them said I was pregnant—except for the most expensive one that claimed to be the most accurate!

I gently wrapped them all back up in the Walmart sacks (gross, I know) to show Andrew, I floated out of that bathroom, and went straight to the baby section. After trying for years, we were finally pregnant, I was going to be a mother, and in that moment I felt such a sense of completion and happiness—it was indescribable! I realize this may sound weird, but it felt like I had completed one of the main things I came here to do, and that was to bring a child into this world.

I picked out a yellow bib that read "I love my Daddy." I grabbed a gift bag, purchased my items, aaaand again, I floated right back out to my car. As I drove back home to my sleeping husband, I remember feeling my hands shaking, as I held tight to the steering wheel. I melted into my seat. I was numb and at the same time I had never felt so alive.

I sat there a minute before going back in; I just wanted to sit in that moment, drink up the fact that I was one with this child inside me. I was the only person on the planet that knew she existed; it was such a profound feeling, such an honor.

It didn't last long, though—my excitement got the best of me, and I quietly snuck back into the house with my pregnancy tests and little gift bag in hand. I was about to tell this guy he was going to be a father...buuuut first I had to pee, again.

Assuming Andrew was still asleep, I rounded the kitchen corner and went straight for the bathroom. Just then Andrew popped out of the laundry room (which was next to the bathroom), scaring me half to death. The gift bag and Walmart bags full of pregnancy tests went flying in the air...and that was how I told him we were pregnant. Showering him with seven peed-on pregnancy tests and a baby bib.

He looked at me, shocked for a moment, surprised I guess that he had spooked me, then he looked on the floor and saw them. I instantly started crying, he joined me.

Later that day, I went to have a blood test done, to confirm that I was pregnant. We were so happy to have our little miracle, but boy, did she have *some* timing (and yes, I knew she was a girl before I actually knew she was a girl).

My intuition was on point: it told me not to spend time and money on getting IVF. From this experience I learned that there was not just one, but two separate voices in my head, my ego and my intuition. My ego has its own agenda and set feelings, and those feelings can not only be completely different and often more negative than those of my intuition but could also lead me to make wrong choices. I was learning to trust a whole new voice. Even though I canceled that IVF appointment, I didn't "feel" like it was in my best interest; I was sad, and it felt wrong—but that was my ego making me feel those things, not my higher voice (intuition). I've been able to use what I learned from this situation over and over again, whenever it feels like my intuition and my ego have ended up at opposite conclusions.

Just a couple weeks after finding out I was pregnant, I would be hit with debilitating morning sickness—actually, all-day sickness! I slept, and I puked, that was it—that's what I did for the next three months of 2013.

I would eventually become too weak to get up and down the stairs to our bedroom and began sleeping on the couch in our living room, with a bowl for puking and a bottle of water by my side. I was the thinnest I'd ever been, which is frightening when you know you are supposed to be supplying nutrients to a baby growing inside of you. The salon project was put on hold until I regained my strength.

By late October I was starting to feel like myself again, and after a few weeks of getting the salon put together (big thanks to my mother, who helped me decorate, paint, and set things up) we opened in late November. We had a beautiful Christmas-themed grand opening. Clients, family, and friends all came out to support me, in what I assumed would be my forever career, it was such a gratifying feeling. We served wine, beer, appetizers, and even had a hot cocoa bar. We gave away a ton of great products, some quick simple services, and samples to everyone in attendance. It was a remarkable evening that filled my cup with love and gratitude.

It was business as usual until the early hours of April 9, 2014. After a long day at the salon, I came home and cleaned the house from top to bottom—I mean, I was literally on my hands and knees cleaning every crevice. I took a hot shower, then finally laid down in bed next to a sleeping husband. You would think I would have just fallen asleep immediately, but that wasn't the case; I put on some true crime TV and tried to find a comfortable position. If you have ever been nine months pregnant, then you know the struggle is real when it comes to getting comfortable. I was all over the place, just as I rolled over into what I thought would be the best position, I felt a pop, followed by a gush!

It was baby time; however, my little girl didn't get the memo; she was in no hurry to arrive. After 20 hours in a hospital bed (six of them actively pushing) my nurse came in and said "Honey, I can't stay any longer, I have to go home, but Holly will be your new nurse and you will love her."

As hour 21 approached, in walked this lady, covered in tattoos, with a black faux-hawk, and colorful cat-eyeglasses. Now, I know what you are thinking—my husband is a tattoo artist, I listen to heavy metal, so her look should be right up my alley, right? Wrong. After spending 20 hours with this sweet little old lady nurse, who was helping me breathe, stay calm, and monitoring my who-ha, the sight of this badass walking in had me scared shitless.

But then she spoke, and all my fears faded away. She was an unbelievable nurse, extremely attentive, and she had me feeling even calmer, than the little old lady with 40 years of experience! I knew this wouldn't be the last time I saw Holly, she just felt so familiar to me. What I didn't know was that Holly the nurse would later play a pivotal role in helping me find my purpose in life.

An hour and a half after arriving, Holly helped us welcome Miss London Drew Buckwalter into the world. London was a name I instantly fell in love with, and after some research, I found out why. London means "fortress of the moon." She was perfect, coming in at seven pounds and seven ounces of adorable sass!

As I stepped into motherhood, I found it harder and harder to want to be anywhere but at home with my baby. At the time, both sets of our parents still had full-time jobs, and we did not trust anyone besides family to care for her. I started taking her to work with me, but as she got older her demands made it really hard to focus on getting through a single service, let alone an entire day of work! I cut down to just a few days a week in the salon, mainly the days Andrew was off so he could be with her, but this put a serious dent in our family dynamic as we were rarely all three together. Finally, I told Andrew I thought it would be best to put her in daycare.

Like always, I did my research, interviewed several facilities, and scheduled tours. One evening, just before we left to see the first daycare, Andrew told me he didn't want to put her in daycare. I couldn't disagree with him; it was exactly how I felt as well.

It felt like I was basically going to have to choose between staying home with London and my business. I was not giving my business the attention it deserved, nor did I feel 100 percent present for my daughter and husband. Being a wife and mother was my only desire.

It occurred to me that these strong feelings to be with my baby full-time may have come, in part, from the fact that my own mother worked when I was a child: she worked hard and a lot, long hours and late nights. I remember missing her, wishing she was able to be home, make dinner, help me with homework, or even just be present so I had a female to talk to. Make no mistake, I had a great childhood, but like most families, both of my parents worked. Oftentimes I would sit alone in my room, crying, wishing she would quit her job or get sick and come home—that sounds terrible, doesn't it? I swore that when I myself had children; I would do whatever it took to make sure I was present after school each afternoon for them. So, I called and cancelled the daycare tour.

It's utterly fascinating to me how the Universe works, providing exactly what you ask it for. The beautiful thing about all of it is that it's actually physics— this is not some woo-woo shit, it is the Law of Attraction, and believe me, my friends, it is real.

Not long after deciding we weren't ready to send our daughter to daycare just yet, two ladies walked into my salon; they were also cosmetologists, and they were looking for something new. They asked me if I was interested in selling the salon—but instead of seeing this as the answer to my prayers, rather than seeing it as a gift from the Universe allowing me become a full-time stay at home mother, my ego took over and I was instantly offended. I hadn't even owned the salon a year yet! I think I felt insulted, because I thought they had assumed that I was not running the salon the way it should be, which was not the case at all—but at the time I couldn't wrap my head around why they thought I'd want to sell it! It's not like I had advertised it.

Looking back, their interest was completely warranted: they were hearing I was not there much and that was true. I had slowly started to phase out my appointments and was focusing solely on managing my salon and its booth renters, making sure they had everything they needed, going in at night after hours and cleaning, running the social media side of things and making sure there was a flow of clients for them—that in itself was a job!

Several days a week, with London strapped to me, I would go hand out fliers around town, just trying to drum up business. I thought if I could keep my stylists happy, I could keep the salon going and also make a little income, until London was older, and I was ready to do hair again. None of my stylists saw how hard I was still working to keep up with the salon, to keep them busy and financially stable, so I'm sure they assumed I was ready to let it go.

But still, that wasn't the case. I politely turned their offer down and instead offered them booths to rent, and to my delight they accepted! I was more than happy to have them there; I just wasn't ready to give up on my dream yet, especially after having worked so hard to get there. They were wonderful women with established clientele, which is something that is hard to come by as a salon owner. I was excited to have stylists with such devotion to their craft by my side.

After just a few months of working with them, their consistent dedication to customers, the salon, and their awesome work ethic floored me. Then, something familiar happened—I heard, in my higher voice, "Sell them the salon." I thought, *you gotta be fuckin kidding me right now.*

If you've ever owned a business yourself and been faced with letting it go, you can likely empathize—it's not an easy choice to make. I had poured so much time, work, love, money, sweat, and tears into this place. In my mind, this was going to be what I did for the rest of my life. If I sold the salon I was giving up everything I had worked so hard for over the last three years. I felt like I was selling my identity to become a stay-at-home mother.

I was so torn over this decision, yet I kept hearing the voice, and it seemed to be getting louder and louder. Every time I would arrive at work, I would hear "sell them the salon."

I realized that it wasn't my passion for doing hair that kept me going, it was my ego and pride, they were the driving force behind me wanting to make this salon such a success. In fact, I started to resent being a stylist altogether; each time I was behind the chair I was giving up precious time with my baby girl, but I felt like I owed it to everyone who helped me along the way to stick it out, and once again, "make them proud." I worried I would be seen as a failure, or lazy, if I gave up so quick—I was more worried about what everyone else would think instead of thinking about what would work best for our family, or what would make me most happy. To this day I am still a recovering people-pleaser, but that's a whole other book! I knew the people that loved me would have told me to sell from day one, had they known how badly I was struggling with this decision.

I scheduled a meeting with the two ladies that originally offered to buy and apologized for not selling it to them months earlier. I explained that their offer had taken me by surprise, and in a way, offended me, because I was trying so hard to give the salon my all. I was trying so hard to figure out how to balance being a new mother and a new business owner.

We settled on a price that would allow me to recoup most of what I had put into the salon. It wasn't easy to hand over my labor of love, but after doing so it felt like a weight had been lifted off of my shoulders. From that day forward I slept better, knowing I was able to focus solely on being the mother I had always dreamt of being, a mother who was present, and completely committed every single day to nurturing her child. I was blessed to have the opportunity to stay home with London and I know that. I understand that being a stay-at-home mom isn't for everyone, but it was the best decision for our little family, and I have never regretted it!

It brought great peace to my heart, knowing that these ladies were going to take care of the salon and love it like I did. The Beauty Bar is still in operation today; it's moved just a block down from the original building, right near the riverfront here in my hometown of Hannibal, Missouri—and yes, this is where I get my hair done! If you stop in, please tell Sam, Allison, Taylor, and Katie hello—any one of them will blow your mind, they are all incredible stylists!

Chapter 6
Salem

Being a stay-at-home mom was wonderful, fulfilling, and most of all, it made me feel complete. I finally felt like things were starting to fall into place; I felt balance within my life for the first time in years. As time went on I started to give more and more tarot readings to friends within the nooks and crannies of my days, mostly while London was napping or after she was down for the night.

As another autumn season crept in, I was feeling drawn to Salem now more than ever. It was always around the Halloween season that I felt the biggest pull: I would get so swept up in the magic of the season, I often found myself daydreaming about going there and what it would be like. I'd make up scenarios in my head, like, *If I left now for St. Louis and booked a flight for 6 p.m., I'd be in Massachusetts by 10 p.m., grab my rental car, drive from Boston to Salem in 15 minutes, find a cheap hotel, and bam! Be ready for a full day of Salem in the morning, and I could be home by Sunday.* Simply put, I became consumed with visiting this place. I was on the mailing list to get a yearly visitors brochure; getting them in the mail was like Christmas for me! I would sit and fantasize about walking the magical streets of Salem, I'd read all about the different kinds of shops they had, and the psychics that practiced there.

Finally, one day, I just decided to pull the trigger. It was time—I didn't have to plan around a work schedule and Andrew was his own boss, so we decided to go for it. Well, I did, and he came along, but he knew how important this was to me and he supported the adventure!

I booked the plane tickets and then took a look at that year's brochure, "Haunted Happenings." There were tons of advertisements for psychics, and I had never had a reading, so I decided that was one thing I definitely wanted to do while there: book a reading with a really good psychic! I found a psychic by the name of Anthony, who worked in shop called Magika. My main focus while there was to find out why I had such a strong pull to this area; maybe he could help shed some light on that. I called and made an appointment for the day we arrived, being careful to only give my first name. I'll be honest, I was a total skeptic: I expected broad statements that could easily relate to anyone, and to be told things about the future based on how old I looked or my gender. Even so, I was still excited just to experience a real reading—and in Salem, no less!

Flying into Boston in October was one of the most beautiful things I had ever seen. The trees created a brilliant ribbon in every shade of red, gold, and orange that flowed throughout the city. When we landed, baby London was sound asleep; she was a perfect little angel the entire flight. We gathered our things, waited by the exit for our stroller, then headed for car rental pick-up (our first time ever renting a vehicle at an airport). It was a bit hectic, being in this huge airport that was completely foreign to us, with a baby who began crying just as it was our turn in line. I don't know why, but they upgraded us from a car to a pimped out white minivan. That thing was awesome!

I was so excited to be there, I was shaking. We were just 15 minutes from making my biggest dream in life a reality! We planned to just use our phone and Google maps to get from the Boston Logan Airport to Salem, but just as I picked up my phone to type in the address to Magika, my phone did one of those Hollywood shutdowns, the kind you see in movies where the screen instantly goes black with a white line in the middle that quickly fades away.

Andrew was approaching an intersection and asking, "Which way, left or right, Britney, LEFT OR RIGHT?" Panicking, I said, "I don't know, I don't know! I'm trying but I think my phone just blew up!" Andrew pulled his out of his pocket, looked at it, and said, "Mine's dead too, what the hell?" I glanced up at the clock of the rental: it was already 3:30 p.m., my appointment with the psychic was at 4 p.m.! I knew Salem was just 15 minutes from the airport, but I still remember thinking, *There, is no way in hell we are going to make it in time, we have no fucking clue where we are going!*

I've never seen a city quite like Boston. Busy is an understatement, the streets were extremely narrow, there were businesses stacked upon businesses, and a Dunkin Donuts on every corner! Everyone seemed to be in a hurry, and there were just as many people walking the streets as there were cars trying to squeeze by each other. This was not a place you wanted to be lost in!

Just as I was about to tell Andrew to pull over to a gas station for directions, we saw a sign with an arrow pointing to the street ahead of us: it read, SALEM 10 MILES. It wasn't your typical green and white reflective sign like you see here in Missouri—it was exactly what you'd expect, an old wooden sign with character and charm, just like Salem itself. I couldn't believe it!

As we approached Salem it was like something out of a movie, the hustle and bustle was gone, and the winding roads gave way to beautiful Cape Cod homes with bright golden trees and white picket fences. I know it sounds crazy, but the magic of Salem was palpable even though we were miles from it! All at once, a sigh of relief and an explosion of excitement hit me. We both looked at each other in amazement and burst into laughter! How in the world were we able to find the Salem exit so fast, in all the chaos that is Boston?

As soon as I saw the "WELCOME TO SALEM EST. 1626" sign, the excitement of a lifelong dream coming true was almost more than I could take. I became deeply emotional; I was both happy and crying—and for some weird unexplainable reason I was also scared. I felt a tightness in my chest that I could not explain. I chalked it up to the excitement and stress of the frantic ride there.

As we pulled into Salem, we faced another directional challenge. We had no idea where Magika was, and we still had zero phone access.

I had looked up the store on the Internet ahead of time, so I knew the general location we were looking for—we needed to find "Pickering Wharf Marina" which was a quaint section of historic shops in Salem, near the sea.

We didn't have to look far, we rolled into Salem and took the first right, turns out that was the right direction. I will never forget that journey. It was as if something bigger than us was guiding Andrew to the exact location we needed to arrive at; there were no bumps, it was so smooth, every turn he "randomly" took led us to exactly where we needed to be. I truly believe it was divine intervention. I needed to be present for this reading; something, or someone helped us arrive right on time for my session with Anthony in that little magical shop on Pickering Wharf.

Parking was a breeze: it just so happened there was a spot right in front of the shop, wide open and waiting for us. I took a big deep breath in, stretched my arms up high, and smiled. It smelled like autumn there, fresh fallen leaves, a crispness in the air, and somewhere off in the distance a fire was going, I could smell just a hint of it. We got our little miss in her stroller and walked up to the shop. I must have looked like a crazy woman to those passing by, I was taking in every sight and smell of the town as we walked to the storefront, not looking in front of myself, but all around—at times nearly tripping!

As I entered I heard a familiar sound: bells on the door, just like I heard the very first time I pushed open the door of The Opened Book back home years ago. The place was overflowing with random whispers and bits and pieces of conversations coming from all different directions of the shop. I think they packed five, maybe six, different psychics in that small parlor—each separated by curtains or fold-out partitions. The shop itself was beautifully decorated with deep hues of gold, red, and purple. Metaphysical books, sage, and Archangel Michael statues lined shelves for purchase.

There was a young woman sitting behind the front desk to greet us. We took a seat in a tiny waiting room—a bit of a reprieve from the hectic airport and wild car ride in. No sooner had we sat down, Anthony walked in and said, "Britney?"

"Oh, yes, that's me, can my husband and baby come with me?" I asked hopefully. He replied, "No, unfortunately their energy will make it hard for me to give you an accurate reading" (something I understand all too well now). I looked back at Andrew and he said, "No big deal, we will chill here, go!"

I followed Anthony back to his reading space: one chair on either side of a small table that was covered in a gold cloth, with tarot cards stacked neatly in the middle. As he began, he said, "Oh, Britney, you have been here before!"

My heart instantly sank. I had picked the wrong psychic—this was my first time in Salem, ever. He was wrong, right off the bat! I said, "No, this is my first time here, I'm just visiting." He looked at me like you would look at a child who has no clue what they are talking about, but it's cute and sweet, so you smile anyway. He said, "No, honey, I mean you have been here in a former life."

I was kind of stunned and shocked, and confused. I knew very little about reincarnation, but I assumed that was what he was referring to. I said, "Oh, well, maybe?"

He went on, "You lived here once before, and your name was very similar to what it is now." He paused, then closed his eyes as if he was listening or waiting for a download of information to come through. His eyes popped back open, he looked at me, studying me for a moment, then he said, "You were Bridget Bishop in a former life. Bridget was the first witch hanged, here in 1692!"

For a split second *I thought ,this dude is full of shit*, then in slow motion everything about my childhood flashed before my eyes: the obsession with witches, love for antique clothing, the deep interest in the Salem Witch Trials as a preteen, the boot dream, the boot dream, OH MY GOD the fucking boot dream!! It all made sense—it all made sense!

He shuffled a worn-looking deck of tarot cards and began to lay them out in front of himself. He began the reading by saying, "Right now someone is making some very big financial plans that involve you." Raising my eyebrows, I said, "Not that I am aware of, but okay." He went on, "You will have one more child, a son, nearly if not exactly 24 months apart from your daughter—and I don't know what your husband does for a living, but he needs to raise his prices immediately."

I chuckled. While I had no intention of having another child at that point and definitely not 24 months from then, Andrew was constantly being told he was pricing his tattoos too low. He is a very skilled tattooist, and it was no secret that he shorted himself often, but that was definitely not something this psychic would know. He went on to make several other predictions for my life, all that would either came true eventually or were already actively happening at that time in my life—but it was what he told me at the very end that left me completely perplexed.

He said, "There is one other very important thing you need to know, Britney. You will become a well-known psychic medium by the age of 28, you need to buy the book *Psychic Self-Defense,* today. We don't sell it here, but I'm sure you can find it online or at another local bookstore—it's very important that you protect yourself."

I nearly fell out of my seat. Fighting back laughter, I said, "Are you sure you are reading those cards right?" He said "Yes, and I'm serious, this is your destiny. When you start seeing triple digits, the Universe will be ready for you, pay attention to the signs." Confused, I said, "Okay."

I thanked him for his reading, and he walked me to the front of the store where Andrew and London were waiting for me. As we stepped out on to the stony walkways of Salem, Andrew said, "Well, we are in your dream city, what would you like to do first?" I said, "I just want to walk the streets and feel the city beneath my feet, I just want to go where I feel pulled, is that okay?" He said, "Let's do it."

As we walked, I told him about the reading, starting with the fact that Anthony had said I was Bridget Bishop reincarnated, that was the part that stuck out to me the most. Then I started to tell him about the parts that didn't make sense, like how I was a part of some big financial plans that were happening right now.

Just then, I remembered I forgot to call my mom and let her know we landed safely. I got my phone out of my purse and tried to turn it on, it worked! I called my mom while standing in front of the beautiful wharf, watching the water move in waves.

She picked up and quietly said, "Britney, did you make it safe?" I said, "Yes, and I just had my reading, it was crazy, you have to hear this!" But before I could get out the next words, she said, "Britney, I am going to have to call you back, Ron and I are with an attorney having our wills written up." *Wait, your wills, as in financial planning?*

I stood there stunned for a moment, as the reality of the connection sunk in. I began to put more stock into the idea that maybe I *had* been here, in Salem, as Bridget Bishop in a former life. So many of my life's unexplained moments as a child would make perfect sense if that were the case—but that was absurd, right? It just wasn't possible...was it?

As we walked the streets of Salem, every single one of my senses were stimulated. I could taste the saltwater from the ocean, and smell food cooking in food trucks and restaurants around us. I saw magical-looking shop windows filled with displays of beautifully adorned witch hats, crystals, wands, and dried flowers. I could hear "The Monster Mash" playing in the background and there was a man dressed as a very creepy clown walking down the street playing a saxophone.

I felt like I was being guided through, by what I don't know, but our leisurely stroll was starting to speed up. I felt a push to keep going, turn left, turn right, walk between these two buildings, go down that alley.

At one-point Andrew finally asked, "Where are we going?" as I began to walk quicker and with more purpose and determination. "I'm not sure," I said. We crossed the street and walked past some vendors selling candied apples, then through some fog that was being generated by fog machines, then past a very ugly, very large witch statue.

As we came out on the other side of the fog, I saw a small cemetery. My mind was racing. On one hand, I thought, *what an odd place for a cemetery, right in the middle of downtown*—but that was it, that's where I wanted to go.

In all my years of reading about Salem, I did not recognize this cemetery at all. A sense of accomplishment came over me as I basically ran toward it, I had my eye on one small stone monument.

As I approached I could see that it read "BRIDGET BISHOP, HANGED JUNE 10, 1692." I fell to my knees.

I'm sure Andrew wanted to tell me, "Get up, you look crazy," but instead he stepped back after reading the stone and eloquently said, "This is the craziest shit I have ever seen in my life."

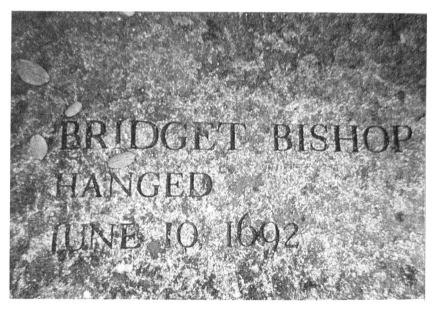

This was the only picture I was able to take while in Salem.

I learned in that moment that coincidences do not exist, and that I was not alone on this journey. I knew that what Anthony had said, would happen one day. I was going to become a psychic medium, and I was Bridget Bishop—I had been here before.

Chapter 7
444

Just as Anthony predicted, I was soon pregnant with my second child, a boy, almost exactly 24 months to the day after my daughter's birthdate. At seven a.m. on April 2, 2016, we entered the delivery ward, and to my surprise we were greeted by a familiar face. Do you remember Holly, the super-cool delivery nurse who came on duty just before I gave birth to my daughter? She was back, and it was so comforting to see her beautiful, bubbly, personality bounce into the room again!

Just like his mama, my son didn't want to do it the easy way. After pushing for hours, the doctor yelling, "Come on, Britney, you've done this before, you can do it again, come on!" the room got silent. The doctor looked at me with a half apologetic, half embarrassed look on his face and said, as if it was no big deal, "Oh, he's sunny-side up! No wonder he's giving Mom so much trouble!" I wanted to punch him in the fucking face. I lost a lot—and I mean a *lot*—of blood during this birth, I thought Andrew was going to pass out; recovery wasn't as easy this time around, but I made it, and officially became a boy Mom to Ledger VanJohn.

Being a mother is the most amazing and rewarding experience I have ever had in my life. I was soaking up every second of my time with them, I probably took, on average, two videos and 50 pictures a day! It's true what they say, they grow up quick!

Shortly after giving birth to Ledger, I began to experience intense visions; It felt like my intuition kicked into overdrive. I have read that many (but not all) psychics begin to experience their abilities only after a life-changing event such as the death of a loved one, a near-death experience, or giving birth.

I also began to see the number 444 quite often. At that point, I had actually forgotten a great deal of the things said in my reading with Anthony two years prior. At first, I thought, *Oh, that's neat.* Then, *Wow, this is weird.* Until I eventually thought, *Okay, what in the actual fuck is going on?* I'm not just talking about the time, or the amount due at the store, or even a poster outside a gas station with a sweet deal on pizza and a coke for $4.44! I was seeing this number everywhere. The decorative numbers at a Hobby Lobby randomly arranged to conveniently display 444 as I walked by, addresses I had to go to or drive past, even on license plates of the cars in front of me! I started to pay close attention to what I was thinking when I saw this number sequence, and nearly every time I saw it, I was thinking about my life's purpose, or going back to work—doing hair again, or something along those lines.

Eventually, I took to social media, and asked friends on Facebook what their thoughts were on seeing this number series multiple times a day. In the comments section, my friend Sheila Scholl posted a link to a numerology site. I clicked on it and began to unravel the mystery.

According to that site and multiple others, the general consensus was that seeing 444 means that you are someone who has strong intuition and who is meant to follow a path of enlightenment. 444 means you are being asked to let go of all your doubts and fears surrounding your ambitions, because you are protected and guided by the angels, you have their support.

In the moments after reading the meaning of that number, it finally registered: I knew *exactly* what this was about! *The reading, seeing triple digits, that's got to be what this is all about—it must be time.* The Universe was gently saying, "Come on out, it's time to fulfill your life's purpose." *Wait, what? Don't I need like some magical training, or Hogwarts, or a mentor?*

I sat down and began to play back the reading in my head, at least what I could remember; all the things that Anthony told me had played out just as he said they would, one by one each prediction came true, that should have been enough for me, but I'm stubborn. I needed more convincing. If I was supposed to follow this path in life, then the Universe, or the angels, or God, or whoever was in charge of this shit was going to have to try a lot harder. Sure, I'd see 444 up to four times a day, but that wasn't enough. Everyone sees that stuff if they are looking for it, right?

On a hot, sticky day in June, Andrew and I had driven down to St. Louis to attend an annual event called the Pagan Picnic, located in Tower Grove Park. The sidewalks are lined with vendors selling crystals and sage, people offering reiki sessions, food, and of course psychics giving tarot readings! It was my first time attending this festival, but the fact that it made me feel at home, was not lost on me; driving a mere two hours to feel completely in my element was totally worth it!

As we walked the strip, a familiar person caught my eye: it was Holly, my delivery nurse! She was with her husband, Ken, and son Kade. She introduced her family to us and then I said with excitement, "Oh, my gosh, are you into this stuff too?" I asked if I could add her on Facebook and did so right then and there. We had a date set up to hang out before I even made it home.

Holly told me about a psychic that lived about three hours from us; she said that she did in-home psychic parties and I instantly knew, I had to have one.

Appropriately set in the month of October, the psychic, Linda (name changed to protect her identity) and her wife, Barb, arrived at my home on Gemini Street. She got started right away reading people in another room—each person with a scheduled time to arrive, most leaving as soon as their appointment was over—while Holly introduced me to her friend Barb. It wouldn't be my turn for a reading until the very end, Linda had a full day of readings to do which meant that I had the whole day to chit chat with Holly and Barb. I instantly felt a connection with her, like we had known each other for years! She was so easy to talk to, full of wisdom and inspirational words; she was the problem-solver for everyone she knew. Holly would always say "Ask Barb" when I would come to her with an issue or decision I was having a hard time with. Over time, Barb and I would develop a beautiful friendship.

Like Holly and Ken, Barb believed in me, more than anyone had ever believed in me before, more than I believed in myself. She told me on numerous occasions that she could see that I had psychic ability and that I needed to use it. This meant a great deal to me, coming from the wife of a professional psychic.

I could feel a change was on the horizon for me, but I wasn't quite sure what that would look like. At the time I had a two-and-a-half-year-old and a six-month-old. I wasn't done being a stay-at-home mom, but I did think often about what I would do when the time came for me to go back to work, which I planned to do when Ledger turned two. I assumed hair, it's good money—but if I was being honest with myself, it did nothing for me. It made me feel like a robot. I wanted a career I was passionate about. I wanted to do something that made me feel like I served a deeper, more fulfilling purpose, something that touched others on an emotional and mental level. I wanted to do something that made a difference in the lives of others on a more profound level. With that being said, let me be clear that's not a stab at hairstylists by any means, I couldn't live without the mad skills of both my hair stylists. The career itself though didn't do anything for me.

One day my mom offered to keep the children so I could go grocery shopping (you know you are a stay-at-home mom when you get excited to go to the grocery store without your children!). So, three hundred bucks later, I was headed back to pick up the kids. I was running late, which typically wouldn't be an issue, except that day my mother had a doctor's appointment she could not be late for.

As I was driving down the highway, my mind went on autopilot. I started thinking about doing psychic readings professionally and imagined what that might look like—but as always my ego quicky shut that down as a possibility. My ego said, *don't even think about it, you will look like a lunatic to everyone in town, it will really upset your in-laws, it will never work out.*

Just then, this tractor pulled out in front of me—the damn thing nearly hit me! It blew my mind that he would do that—like, just wait five seconds for me to pass, dude! I was already running late, and now I was stuck behind this slow-ass excavator tractor thing.

I looked in my rearview mirror and saw a long line of cars behind me, then looked back at the tractor, that's when I saw it. I shit you not, there was a black, spray-painted 444 on the back of this tractor! I was literally forced to slow down and look at 444 for about five miles! I could not believe my eyes; it took my breath away.

I remembered what I was thinking when it showed up: intuitive readings, being a psychic, doing this professionally. It was such a surreal moment for me. I took a deep breath, adjusted myself in my seat, sat straight up, and (not knowing who or what I was even talking to) said, "Okay, I'm listening, what's next?"

Chapter 8

Didn't See That Coming...

I was in the kitchen getting lunch ready for the kids when my phone lit up
with a text from Barb informing me that she and her wife would be hosting a
psychic fair and spirit circle, and she wanted me to come check it out. I'd been to
many psychic fairs by this point, but a spirit circle was something new for me.
Because it was three hours away, I had no interest in going, but if this had been
local I would have been there in a heartbeat! I told Barb that I didn't have a sitter
which was the truth—but I also didn't really have anyone I wanted to reach out to
on the other side, and I really didn't want to spend the money on a ticket, gas,
and eating out, not to mention six hours of driving in one day. She said she
understood, and that was that. But it wasn't, because it never is.

Minutes later, my phone rang—it was my mother, who said she missed the
kids and wanted to take them that Friday and keep them overnight. I stood there
like an idiot, speechless. After the phone call ended with my mother, I
immediately got another text from Barb: "If you happen to find a sitter for the

kids, I want to pay for your ticket to the spirit circle." *Ooookay... I guess this is what's next.*

I was told by my friend Holly that there would be a really good psychic named Sherri there; she suggested that I get a reading from her. So that was my plan: find this Sherri, get a reading during the one-on-one portion of the event, stay for the circle thing, make Barb happy, then get back home.

What I did not expect was how amazing my reading with Sherri would be! I was extremely impressed: her style was unique, detailed, and spot-on. More importantly, that reading would be the start of another beautiful relationship in my life.

After my private reading with Sherri, I found Barb, she introduced me to a few of her friends, and by that time the one-on-one portion of the fair was wrapping up. Barb's wife announced that we would be moving into the spirit circle and asked that we all grab a seat. I sat in the very back; there was about 20 people there. It was a small space, but perfect for this type of event: chairs were set up theater-style, with four chairs at the front of the room for the mediums.

I took a deep breath and looked around the room. *Why am I so nervous? It's not like I'm not reading these people.* There really wasn't anyone that I longed to reach out to on the other side; I wasn't hoping for a connection. I assumed it must be everyone else's energy that was making me so antsy. When I think back on this story it makes me giggle—there were still so many things about my ability that I had yet to understand and discover, being an empath was one of them.

I'm taking the time to point this out because I am sure many of you have been in a similar situation, where you felt some sort of way but had no reasonable explanation for why you felt that way. Congratulations, you're an empath! Learning how to control that ability isn't easy; it's taken many years for me to learn how to identify what are my own feelings, and what are those of someone else that is near me at the time. Unfortunately, I have very little advice for this; learning to stay grounded and present helps. Simply, being aware and staying in touch with your own feelings helps too.

But, this was before I had even heard the term empath. The lady next to me was so nervous she couldn't stop fidgeting; the look on her face was pure despair, it made me want to cry. I could tell she was so badly hoping for a message, but so was everyone else in that room. It reminded me a lot of my pageant days, when each contestant is standing on a stage, praying that their name will be called, praying that they are the new Miss Whatever—the energy was that intense!

Linda sat between two people at the front of the room, Sherri being one of them. She began to channel Spirit; she would start by describing a number of things about the spirit she was connecting with like how they passed, what they looked like, or what their personality was like while here on Earth. She would then ask the audience if this made sense to any of them.

Sometimes someone would raise their hand right away, confident that it was, in fact, their loved one coming through. Other times people sat silent, with a look of confusion, trying to digest what Linda was saying. I could tell they were trying to piece the information together. Most of the evidence was spot-on; however, some were unsure and could not confirm details, simply because the sitter (the person being read) simply did not know the correct answer to the question in the first place or the just couldn't remember.

I sat up in my seat; I was intrigued. It was in that moment that I began to see, in my mind—just as you would picture your mother, brother, or child in your head—a beautiful woman, with blond hair that was blowing in the wind. And this was peculiar: there was water flying up everywhere, like water was being sprayed at her, and she had a big, beautiful smile on her face. I couldn't make out what she was doing just yet, but I thought this may have something to do with someone in this room. It was completely bizarre—who just pictures a woman they have never seen before in their mind—while awake?!

I looked at Barb, who was sitting next to me, leaned into her, and I whispered in her ear what I was seeing. She looked back at me and in a hasty and matter-of-fact way said, "Well, say something!"

I looked at her like she was crazy! First of all, I had no clue why I was seeing this or what it meant; second, this was Linda's event, and I didn't want to upset her or throw her off in some way; and third, I felt it would be rude to interrupt them.

Barb continued to nudge me with her elbow; she gave me that *Listen to me, damn it* look. I felt a sense of calm and confidence wash over me. It was like I stepped out of the hard shell that was my ego and into a soft, warm, comforting bed, where there was no judgment and nothing to fear. I often look back on this moment, even today, as my moment of transition from who I knew myself to be into who I was meant to be—my guides made it an absolutely beautiful and safe evolution.

I raised my hand. I have no fucking clue why, but it got Linda's attention. She said, "Yes, Britney, does this fit for you?" She must have been bringing someone through while I was spacing out, because I had no clue what she had been saying.

All of a sudden it just came out: "Um…I am seeing this really pretty lady, with blond hair…it's blowing in the wind, and I see water all around her. She has a beautiful smile, and she's pointing to her nose right now…."

The silence was unbearable. For just a second (although it seemed like an hour to me) you could have heard a pin drop in that room. I could see confusion on the faces of everyone turning to look at me in the back of the room. I'm sure they all thought I was bat-shit crazy. Then, two women in the very front row let out what sounded like a gasp of air mixed with whimpers.

One of the ladies spoke: "That was my niece, she just passed in a waterskiing accident. She was beautiful, with long blond hair and a big beautiful smile, and she always said she wanted to get a nose job because she hated her nose."

I was floored, almost unable to move. I opened my mouth, but no words came out; I guess I was processing everything she had just said. The water, and the nose job reference, both made sense.

I managed to get out, "Well, her nose looks great to me, but now I am seeing my children…I'm feeling so proud of my own kids right now, I just want to talk about my children."

I said to myself, *What the fuck is this? If this was supposed to be like this woman's spirit coming through, why would she make me see* my *children? These people don't care about me or what I am feeling or that I miss my kids. What is happening?!*

The aunt started to shake her head as if she understood this reference, and said, "She left four children behind." The feelings I was experiencing, I realized then, were to help me understand who this woman was: bringing up my children made sense because it was a huge part of who she was. I was slowly starting to put it all together.

After my brief encounter with the beautiful blond, I went on to read a few more people that night. One spirit showed me grape jelly—it came through just as any other thought would, but with the presence of male energy behind it. Like, I felt manly, I felt stronger, bigger, I just knew, instinctively, that this was coming from a man. Then I began to crave grape jelly.

I asked if there was anyone who could connect with a male showing me grape jelly. The lady sitting next to me let out a giggle and said yes, and it escapes me now how she was related to him (I think she was his wife), but I remember through laughs and tears, she explained that while alive he was obsessed with grape jelly, he was known to put it on absolutely everything, she said people knew him by his love of grape jelly, he used to carry around those little square tubs of it you get at restaurants.

While my readings that night were elementary, to say the least, witnessing a wave of peace and closure wash over these grieving individuals made the awkwardness I felt while relaying the evidence all worthwhile. They now had something to hold onto: a bit of closure, and proof that their loved ones were still with them and that life truly does exist after death. I had never before been able to make an impact like that on anyone.

After the circle ended, most everyone left, some stuck around to chat. Once we were alone, with an "I told you so" look, Barb told me how proud she was of me. I knew in that moment that she had been called to make me fully aware of this ability; she was there to aid in building my confidence. I told her I would forever be grateful for the gift she gave me that night, and I thanked her for being the bridge between myself and the spirit world.

As I pulled out of town that night to start the three-hour trek home, my mind was racing, and my adrenaline was through the roof. I was literally talking out loud to myself: "I can't believe this; I can't fucking believe this shit! I've had this ability all along and never even knew it. I missed it, this whole time I completely missed it! There have been so many times throughout my life that I've

experienced exactly what I did in that room! Holy fuck, this is insane!!

"Wait, what is that? Is that—MOTHERFUCKER!! Are you serious right now?"

Apparently in my adrenaline-fueled state I was unaware that I was doing 68 in a

35. I wasn't even aware I was driving through a town, for crying out loud!

"This is some bullshit!" Yep, I was being pulled over by a cop.

Chapter 9

Blocked

In between cleaning up spilled Cheerios, breastfeeding, and wiping baby butts, I spent the next few days contacting my small circle of friends and family that I knew were open to my abilities. Despite knowing each sitter, I was still able to make genuine connections with the spirits of people I had never met before, telling them things I could not have possibly known. Doing these mediumship readings, helped me build the confidence I needed to begin to look for other avenues to test my psychic and mediumistic abilities.

I think it's important for me to note that I never set out to be a medium, or even a psychic for that matter. In fact, the time in my life that this all came to fruition couldn't have been worse. I was a sleep-deprived, stay-at-home mother, raising two kids that were still in diapers. Most of the time my mind was focused on just getting through each day, but my intrigue and curiosity for my "newfound" ability filled me with the stamina I needed to continue to grow, explore, and educate myself. I wanted to know everything, I wanted to challenge myself by reading outside of my comfort zone.

A friend of mine told me about a psychic fair being held in Columbia, Missouri, at a small metaphysical shop. I read up on the requirements for the fair: clients paid $10 for a ticket at the store, then gave the ticket to the psychic of their choice for a reading. At the end of the day the psychics would turn their tickets in for $5 each; the store kept $5 per reading for hosting the fair.

I decided to give it a try. What did I have to lose? Maybe this was what I needed to do to prove to myself once and for all that I really could do this. I was so nervous, it felt like reading strangers was really going to be the next big step for me. Barb was cheering me on, via text, she gave me so much motivation and confidence to do this, she said, "You are going to blow your own mind!" On the day of the fair, I walked in and was greeted by that familiar smell—if you have ever been in a metaphysical shop you know the one I'm talking about. For me, metaphysical shops are like the grown-up version of a book fair! Do you remember the excitement of going to the book fair as a kid with five bucks in your pocket, wanting to buy everything?!

The shop had random open tables set out for each reader to sit at, but there wasn't much privacy or much room for that matter—we could all literally hear each other talking while reading our sitters. There was no information about us given by the shop associates, so people just had to use their own intuition when it came to picking a reader (fitting, right?). I sat down at an open table, pulled out my notebook, pen, and tarot cards, and was ready for business! Almost immediately I had my first client! A tall young man, with dark curly hair and a beautiful complexion. He had glasses on, was wearing a rather mature-looking sweater, and had a girlfriend waiting for him off to the side.

This was the first male not related to me that I had ever read, and he looked nothing like my idea of what a man that would want a psychic reading would look like, he just looked so, normal. I told him I was both a psychic and a medium, and explained the difference, and then asked him if he would like a psychic reading or a mediumship reading. He said, "Psychic, please."

I got my tarot deck out and began to shuffle my cards, explaining to him that I would intuitively pull three cards for him: one for his past, one for his present, and one for his future. I said, "I will then tell you what I have seen in your past and ask that you just say yes, that is accurate, or no, that does not make sense. I'll then do the same with the next card, only it will pertain to what you are presently experiencing in life—again just a simple yes or no, please do not elaborate. Once I have read those two cards I will then read your future card." I learned very early on, through trial and error, that the less I know about a person and their situation, the more accurate their reading tends to be. This keeps my ego from butting in and assuming things, instead of just following my intuition, which tends to be far more accurate. He nodded that he understood.

I pulled his three cards. Interestingly enough, each card had something to do with financial situations. Lucky for him, each card got progressively better in terms of finances. I told him that in his past I saw that he was attracted to working with numbers—maybe an accountant or a math teacher? He said, "Yes, that makes sense."

"In your present I see that you are still on that same path in life, working with numbers—however this card shows me that you are having a hard time making a decision, in reference to the numbers and or finances in your life."

"Yes, that also makes sense," he said.

I said, "Your future card shows me that not only do you continue to work with numbers, but you will become very wealthy doing so."

With a big smile he said, "Well, that's what I was wanting to hear. I have been having a hard time deciding if I should stick with my current major or if I should change tracks." The other major, he said, would have nothing to do with numbers and would result in him making less per year, but it would be easier on him, require less school, and allow him to stay in Columbia. He said, "Thank you very much, this was exactly what I needed!" The reading obviously had far more detail, but that was it in a nutshell.

I ended up doing more readings than any other reader there that day—I have no clue why, but I wasn't complaining. At one point there was a line wrapped around the store of people waiting to get a reading from me. That was a lot of pressure, but I found that despite the stress of people waiting on me (and my energy slowly draining) all of the readings were incredibly accurate. Countless times that day I was asked, "How can I find you to get another reading?" "Do you have a website?" "Do you have a Facebook page?" I didn't realize until then that I had no way for these people to reach me for future readings without giving them all my personal phone number, and I wasn't comfortable doing that.

I was still too scared to come out with this locally. I was concerned about being viewed as some kind of devil worshiper, or a stay-at-home mom that went off the deep end because her children drove her mad (dramatic, I know)—but Barb encouraged me to just create a Facebook page that didn't have my name or photo on it, where clients could communicate with me and get information. I called it Blessings Beyond Belief.

With each and every reading I did, I was slowly proving to myself that this was real. The interest in readings, and the groups of people, just kept getting bigger and bigger, until eventually they were less of a group and more of an audience. I was learning to trust what Spirit and my guides were telling me to say, and I was building up the confidence needed to fulfill my life's purpose as a platform medium. I was proving, to myself just as much as I was to my sitters and the rest of the world, that spirit communication is not only real, but that I could do it.

Life was going great, and I was getting ready to book my very first live group reading, you remember that one in LaPlata from the first chapter, when I got a text from Barb saying that she and Linda were getting a divorce. I was shocked. To me Barb and Linda were that couple everyone looked up to; From day one I noticed how they were with each other and thought, *Man, I just want it to be like that for Andrew and me.* Barb had never mentioned a single issue between the two of them before. I was floored, and so confused—how did I not pick up on that?

She said she just wasn't comfortable talking about it until she knew for sure it was over, and I get that. When you are the friend everyone goes to for advice, it's not easy to admit that you too, have issues of your own.

Because of this, I quickly became one of her trusted confidantes, and eventually, her personal psychic. We were texting nearly every hour of the day. She began to lean on me more and more, and I was more than happy to be there for the woman who was always there for everyone else, myself included.

One day she asked me if there was another woman in Linda's life. I said, "No, but there will be, and her name is Diana" (name changed to protect the identity of those involved).

Barb adamantly denied that Diana was even a possibility; she told me that this woman was a dear friend of hers, as well as Linda's, that she was straight, and she was married to a man. She said, "Diana would never do that to me."

Three weeks after this conversation, Linda came out on social media about her new love. She was, in fact, officially in a relationship with Diana.

From that moment on Barb would ask me to give her intuitive advice nearly every day, sometimes multiple times a day. This wasn't something that bothered me, it just made me feel a bit overwhelmed from time to time (again, remember: Mom, toddler, baby, breastfeeding, starting a new business that was already overwhelming in nature, in addition to taking care of my home and occasionally helping Andrew out on busy days at the tattoo shop).

I started to worry about being too close to the situation to be an effective psychic for Barb. What if my visions were tainted by my growing concern for Barb's emotional state, not to mention what I already knew about the situation? The last thing I wanted to do was give someone false information.

I asked Barb if we could focus more on our friendship and less on her love life. Looking back, I feel that was an absolutely selfish thing for me to ask of her. The stress I was experiencing had more to do with learning how to balance all the new things in my life, and less to do with her daily text messages.

I won't lie, I did feel, at times, like I was being taken advantage of (as I am sure she did too, from her circle of friends reaching out for daily guidance) but again, looking back, it was my own fault. I should have just told all my new clients to make an appointment, instead of allowing them to solicit free advice at the drop of a hat; then I would have been able to focus more on Barb, without getting so overwhelmed. I didn't need her the way she needed me at that time, so why did I feel so comfortable telling her I needed a break from daily relationship advice and predictions?

Her response to my request was so eloquent: she said she completely understood and apologized and asked me how I was handling life. We had a good conversation that day; it felt like our friendship hit a new level.

Then, nothing. I didn't hear from her for five days, then a week. I assumed she was upset with me, then I got offended, like maybe she only wanted to be my friend for readings. But I knew better, that wasn't like Barb, plus she had many other psychic friends that could read for her.

Finally, two weeks later, I get a message from Barb wishing me a Happy Mother's Day, followed by, "I know you asked me to not ask you so much about my love life, but I was wondering if I could get an in-person reading. I'll drive to you; I really need this."

I said, "Yes, absolutely!" I didn't even care that she wanted a reading, I was just relieved that we were talking again—but because I was driving at the time that I received her text, I told her I would look at my schedule and send her a few open dates to choose from once I got home.

When I got home, I went straight to the kitchen to prepare dinner, then started cleaning the house, getting the kids ready for bed...and so, Sunday passed, and I forgot to message her back. Then came Monday, another busy day, shuffling the kids from grandparent to grandparent so I could get a full day of readings in. By Tuesday night I was knee-deep in landscaping my front yard. Pulling weeds, removing rocks, trimming back roses, I was on autopilot, when all of a sudden I felt something from Barb: an uneasy feeling, almost like a cry for help.

Fuck! Barb! I totally forgot to message her back! I ran into the house to look for my phone. I sent her a message that said, "You will be the one driving three hours to get this reading, so you pick the day and time, I will make it work. I'm so sorry I forgot to text you back, I love you!"

I put my phone down, feeling better about having made contact with her. I went back outside to pack up my supplies and call it a night. I assumed there would be a message from Barb waiting for me when I got back inside. I took off my sweaty clothes, hopped in the shower, and then sat down with my phone, ready to read Barb's message, but there was no message, no response at all.

This was totally out of character for Barb. She has the best phone etiquette of anyone I have ever met. She always texts back, almost immediately. *Maybe she's upset with me; it took me too long to get back to her.* I felt like such a shitty friend. I remember checking my phone the rest of the night for that message, but nothing came, so I went to bed.

At about 1:30 the next afternoon, my phone rang. It was Holly, she said, "Are you sitting down?" I responded "Yes, why, what's going on?"

"They found Barb dead in her bed this morning, she's gone."

There was a sting in my nose, I instantly felt the burn of tears forming, rolling out of my eyes like a tsunami. It felt like I had been punched in the stomach. I remember screaming, and cussing, and my hands would not stop shaking. This was the first time in my life that I could ever remember feeling despair. I wanted to throw up.

How did I not see this coming? Was this what I felt last night? Had she already passed when I sent that message? I went into my text messages; she had an iPhone, and had it set to tell the sender if she had "read" the message or not. It was never opened; she never got that last text message I sent.

I've never experienced confusion quite like I did after Barb's death. I put my tarot cards and my mediumship notebooks away; I didn't want to see them again. I thought, If I can't save someone I love, what's the point of this ability? I felt betrayed by my guides and the spirit world. I didn't answer a single message on Blessings Beyond Belief for over three months.

The friendship between Holly, Sherri, and myself grew deeper that summer. It took countless conversations with them before I even had the desire to read again. I remember them both telling me over and over again, "Britney, you were blocked from this, you were blocked from knowing what was going to happen." I found some comfort in that, even though I didn't fully understand it—but it helped me come to terms with feeling like I should have been able to save her. It made me understand that no matter how intuitive I am, there will always be situations out of my control, and apparently that was something I needed to learn.

It finally registered with me, exactly where I stood in the grand scheme of things. Barb's passing opened my eyes to the fact that I would get what they give me, nothing more, and nothing less. I would know what they needed me to know, not necessarily what I wanted to know. It made me understand on a deeper level that we are all just students of the Universe, here to learn these hard lessons through our own individual human experiences, and I am no exception to that. Being psychic doesn't make me bulletproof, it doesn't make me a superhero, or give me an edge up on anyone for any reason, if anything it makes me more human than most, because I feel things on a much deeper level.

Barb's passing forced me to feel a level of pain I had never experienced in my life up until that point—a kind of pain that many of my clients feel on a daily basis. I love that even in spirit, Barb is making me a better medium, a more emotionally connected and understanding medium, and a better human being in general. She still shares her wisdom with me today; I am guided by her often. She motivates me, picks me up when I am down, and even knocks me down a notch when I need that too. I love you Barb. Thank you for helping me become who I am today.

Rest in Peace My Beautiful Friend

Barbara Jean Case

June 27, 1961-May 17, 2017

"We are so lightly here, it is love that we are made, and in love we disappear..." —Leonard Cohen

Chapter 10

Stella Gets Her Groove Back

Life doesn't always turn out the way we expect it to, even for a psychic. By 2018 it had become clear to me that things were shifting within my marriage. It was like we were living in two different chapters of the same book, with hundreds of pages in between us, and no matter how hard I tried to turn the pages of time back, I just couldn't find him. Aside from Barb's death, coming to this realization was the hardest thing I have ever been faced with to date.

Andrew and I separated in October 2018 and divorced a year later. Learning how to navigate the difficult parts of divorce and co-parenting seems at times to be my soul's biggest challenge this time around. I think many would assume that when you get a divorce it's because you couldn't learn how to understand each other, but for me, agreeing on the divorce meant that we had finally begun to understand each other for the first time in years.

Andrew and I are committed to maintaining our friendship and co-parenting the two beautiful souls we've created. It's not always easy, though, and I hope that in reading this, should you be in the same situation, you know that even for someone who's devoted to peace, love, and positivity, it's still super hard. Being a human is hard, feelings are hard, maintaining self-control with your words and actions are hard, but nobody's perfect. Give yourself some credit and understand that you are not alone—and remember, positive change doesn't always feel good at first.

I appreciate the many years and experiences we had together, and I would not change a thing. After all, our relationship was a part of who I've become, and I am really proud of who I am today—and so, we forge on in this thing called life still united in parenthood and friendship.

Picture this: a 31-year-old single mother of a two, with a brand-new, spiritually based business as my sole form of income, located in the Bible Belt of America, faced with the daunting task of explaining to possible future landlords that my main source of income is being a voice for the spirit world?

These gray haired, 60- and 70-year-old men were so nice, up until the moment they asked me what I did for a living. After that it was like they couldn't get me out of their rentals soon enough. Every single one of them looked at me like I was fucking nuts. I went to house, after house, after house—and eventually stopped bringing the kids to view potential homes. They would get so excited about "our new house," I got sick of feeling my heart break every time I heard

"Dis is gonna be my room, okay Mommy?!" I couldn't stand the thought of disappointing them again. Most house showings ended with me crying in the car on the way to pick up the kids, because I knew by the look on the landlord's face they would not be calling me back. Even in 2019, to most people in this part of the world, my profession simply wasn't looked at as a profession, but as a hobby at best.

To this day, when people ask what I do, it's typically followed by, "Oh, so do you do that full-time or just on the side?" or my favorite, "Is that all you do?" It can be incredibly disheartening, but I am convinced that these people are put in my path for a reason—not just as a test of my strength and loyalty to the spirit world, but to open these individuals up, to educate them and expose them to the normalcy of what we do, as mediums and intuitives.

Remember back to the first chapter of this book when I told you, the one thing I was positive about was Spirit's ability to assist and provide for you? That was the promise they made to me, and they continued to do so. A beautiful little home situated on a golf course landed right in my lap.

Almost immediately after my separation, I went from doing a total of four mediumship demonstrations in one year to 35 the following year. Events began selling out and as far as private readings went, I was faced with more work than I could handle.

I was able to move out of my tiny second-floor office and into an office with a studio, where I could do events and teach classes, in addition to private readings. It felt amazing to be confidently doing what I felt I was put on this Earth to do. It was like I had busted through the chains of my own ego and found true freedom.

But there was still one chain left, one more chain to bust free from, a chain I carried around my body every single day, quite literally. I wouldn't realize it until well over a decade after the rape but the emotional and mental wounds that were created from that violation (and never talking about) had spilled over into physical ones. They haunted me so much that, at some point, I decided I never wanted to have my picture taken again. This little girl that landed on Earth feeling like she had a message to share with the world, never wanted to be looked at again. I even went so far as to pity models, because in my own fucked-up mind, the only thing that being a model would get you is being disrespected, taken advantage of, and raped (extreme I know, but I'm telling you like it was).

I slowly started to "cure" those wounds with food. I ate my feelings. I ate, and I ate, and I ate, eventually developing a very unhealthy relationship with food.

By the time I realized what I had done to myself, I was 222 pounds. I was disgusted, and disappointed in myself, and worst of all, I was embarrassed to leave my house. I avoided cameras like the plague (or should I say Covid?). I routinely laid in bed and looked at old modeling pictures of myself, which led to crying for hours and lots of Oreos.

Stepping into this new career, where I was often onstage, escalated these negative thoughts about my physical appearance. For years I would say, *who cares what people think about me, I am who I am*—but this wasn't about other people, this, was about me, and I didn't like me. How could I inspire others if I was a letdown to myself? How could I expect others to respect my work if I didn't respect who I was? It started to feel like I was living a lie.

The moment I realized I was not living an authentic life; I knew something had to be done. As a certified life coach, weight loss was a topic that came up often in my sessions. So, I asked myself, *what would you tell your clients?* I would tell them, *Heal the emotional wounds first, then move on to the physical obstacles standing in your way.*

Then it clicked for me. I had been going about losing weight wrong all along. I was trying to heal a physical issue before healing the root cause of it: the emotions behind the issue. This was a lot like trying to cook a nice meal in a dirty kitchen. It's much easier to clean the kitchen up first and then cook, instead of lacking counter space, having to work around dirty dishes, clutter, and food that should be put away in the appropriate cabinets. Plus, it's much more enjoyable to cook in a clean space, isn't it? The same applies in this situation.

Clearing your emotional cache (doing the work, the hard stuff, removing negative pent-up emotions and any pain that is keeping you from living peacefully, by any means necessary, be it through counseling, EFT, hypnosis, whatever method is most effective for you) is just as important as changing the oil in your car before it blows up! It is linked back to good mental and emotional health, as well as mental clarity, but so many overlook this aspect of healing. Your issues could lie within your love life, career, unresolved trauma, or any other personal struggle—but whatever the physical issue is, you must heal the emotional wound that caused it first.

Don't get me wrong—you will soon read that physical exercise and cutting out carbs and sugar were pivotal in my own weight loss journey, and that was also important. But I feel we truly need to start within.

Think about all the people you know that go through a breakup or divorce and then lose a substantial amount of weight. More than likely, for many of them, their desire to consume food in an unhealthy manner was probably fueled by stress, unhappiness, depression, or other issues within the relationship. Once they removed themselves from the root cause of their emotional wounds, the weight basically "fell off." They had less desire to eat because they were no longer feeding an emotional wound (granted, this is not always the case, but for me it was and maybe this will resonate with someone out there that needs to hear this right now).

Now, I am not saying go get a divorce if you can't lose weight; that is just one example of how your emotional and mental state can affect you physically. In fact, I didn't lose weight as a result of my divorce at all—I actually continued to gain weight after my divorce, which is why this all makes so much sense. My failing marriage wasn't the reason I was eating so much (although, I thought for many years it was); it wasn't the root cause of my emotional pain. The root cause was the sexual assault, something I hadn't yet delt with. I never really held any kind of space for what happened to me; I just went on for years pretending like it didn't happen, I never truly acknowledged it. I was able to identify the main cause of my weight gain through EFT, a practice my friend Kelly Howe introduced me to.

I'd like to break down the process of EFT for you here, so that you can better understand it and maybe give it a try!

Tapping, or EFT (Emotional Freedom Technique), is an alternative treatment for physical and emotional pain and stress that is based on the traditional Chinese medicine practice of acupuncture. EFT developer Gary Craig believes a disruption in energy is the cause of all negative emotions and pain. Tapping has been used and proven to treat people with everything from PTSD and anxiety disorders to stress and out-of-control cravings (as a bonus, there are no known negative side effects to EFT!).

I had heard a bit about EFT from others over the years, but I never really tried it until one day the Universe literally put it right in front of my face. As I walked into a room filled with people all waiting and hoping to receive a message from a loved one in spirit, I noticed a woman sitting in the front row. I felt connected to her, but I had no clue who she was.

She pulled me aside after the event and introduced herself as Kelly Howe; she explained that she was an EFT coach and asked if I would be interested in trading an EFT session for a private reading. I will admit, I was on the fence about this, but I was struggling so much with back pain and my weight at that time that I was willing to try anything.

After just one session with Kelly, my back pain went from a 10 to a 3, and I was an instant believer! While I highly suggest using a coach for your first few EFT sessions, this is most definitely something you can do on your own, in the comfort of your own home at no cost to you. YouTube has a plethora of helpful videos and guided sessions.

Because I fell in love with how quickly and effectively tapping worked for me (keep in mind, everyone is different and all issues are not the same, some may take more than just a few sessions to achieve effective results), I started slowly implementing EFT into my everyday life.

Not long after my first session, I decided to try using it on my weight issues. I wanted to identify the root cause of my weight gain and try to better understand why I was struggling so hard to lose it.

Here is a breakdown of what an EFT session looks like. Step One: Identify the issue you are struggling with. For me, it was my weight. Step Two: Test the intensity level of said issue. In order to be sure that you are making progress with tapping, you must assess the intensity of the issue (your current emotional or physical pain level related to the identified issue) before you begin. Use a scale of 1 to 10: 1 being not intense at all, 10 being overwhelmingly intense. For me, my weight issues (and how I felt about myself because of them) were at a 10. Step Three: Establish a phrase that explains what you are trying to address. This is also known as the "setup" step. The most common setup phrase and the one that I prefer to use is "Even though I have this [fear, problem, weight issue,] I deeply and completely accept myself. Step Four: Begin the tapping sequence. Often while doing the sequence you may actually see a vison in your mind of exactly what the root cause of this pain is, so be on the lookout for that— however, you do not need to have a vision or thought come to mind in order for this process to work.

There are 12 major meridians that are each linked and correspond to different organs in the body. Typically, EFT only focuses on nine of them, they are as follows: the side of the hand, which corresponds with the small intestine meridian; the top of the head, which corresponds with the governing vessel (up the spine and over the head, stimulates emotional regulation of the mind); the eyebrow, which corresponds with the bladder meridian; the side of the eye, which corresponds with the gall bladder meridian; under the eye, which corresponds with the stomach meridian; under the nose, which, like the top of the head, also corresponds with the governing vessel; the chin, which corresponds with the central vessel (central nervous system); the inside of the collarbone, which corresponds with the kidney meridian; and finally, under the arm, which corresponds to the spleen meridian. You will recite the setup phrase you have chosen at each tapping point, and you will repeat the entire sequence three times.

Step Five: Once you have competed the sequence, you will once again rate the intensity level. The idea is to continue treatments until you are at a level zero, as far as intensity goes.

Again, after just one session (and I should note, I don't think one session will be all that's needed for most people) of EFT, I was able to clear away years of intense pain and negative emotions surrounding my weight.

Once again, Identifying the root cause of your emotional wound is imperative to success in healing a physical wound. You will feel so much better starting your physical journey without having to carry all of the negative weight of past emotional issues. You will have less setbacks, a clearer mind, and fewer bad days moving forward; in fact, using a process like EFT or hypnosis can greatly speed up the healing process, allowing you to heal your physical pain or issues even quicker!

The mental clarity and healing that came from identifying the root cause of my weight gain, made me realize that somewhere deep inside my subconscious mind, I had decided I needed to punish myself for being stupid, for using a fake ID, for wearing a short dress, for drinking underage, for being somewhere I shouldn't have been. I believed that by making myself unattractive through weight gain, I would be protected from something like this ever happening again. I gained the weight because in my mind I was a bad person for not following the rules, and I subconsciously felt that I deserved to look like this—that I needed to look like this.

After using EFT to let go of the pain that I had carried around for over a decade, I was now able to move on to the physical obstacles—I felt a deep, burning desire to move my body! The motivation I had been lacking for years had finally showed up!

I made an appointment with my doctor about how to proceed with effective, long-lasting weight loss results, I ran twice a day, and cut down on my consumption of carbs and sugar. It wasn't easy, let me tell you—I nearly died the first time I got on that damn treadmill—but my heart and mind began to look at exercise and eating healthier as a way of loving myself and treating myself better.

Relying on cookies and lying-in bed began to feel more like a punishment, and there it was—*there it was*—the clarity I was telling you about!

Today I am happy to say I am down nearly 80 pounds of emotional trauma, fear, anxiety, and depression, and I have kept that off for four, going on five years now. Something tells me continuing to keep it off won't be a problem, considering I did the emotional work and healed the reason I felt the need to pack it all on in the first place!

Here is a side by side of my emotional, mental, and physical transformation. I hope this inspires you in the same way that so many others have inspired me with their before and after's!

I'm so proud of this accomplishment, mainly because I know that my children witnessed this process, they watched Mom stay strong. They knew I wanted to be healthier not just for myself but also for them, and that's what I did. I love taking pictures with my babies now, I love running after them, going on new adventures and long walks with them.

Speaking of my babies—my moon (London) and my sun (Ledger)—they are now nine and seven and thriving! I will say, though, that I have my work cut out for me. I'm often asked if naturally strong psychic and/or mediumship abilities are genetic, and my children are living proof that they are! London has shown many signs of strong intuition and heightened psychic abilities.

One of my earliest memories of this was when she was just four years old. Her father had a pizza-maker in the kitchen of his tattoo shop, as getting away for lunch could sometimes be hard for him. He decided one evening to pop a pizza in and bring it home, so I didn't have to make dinner.

He arrived home, walked in the door, and my tiny toddler looked at him and said, "Daddy, where's the pizza?" I looked at him, puzzled, as he had not told me he was planning to bring a pizza home. His face was stricken with confusion and disbelief. He then yelled, "Oh my God! I left the pizza oven on with a pizza in it! I'll be right back!"—and out the door he went! After he returned home (sadly with no pizza, that was the last one), he explained that he wanted to bring home pizza (my all-time favorite food), but he was in such a hurry to get home that he had completely forgot about his plan to surprise us with dinner. Had London not reminded him, the repercussions of this could have been detrimental to his shop.

London's ability to read someone telepathically, at just six years old, was incredible! She still to this day will bring up conversations she was never a part of, that took place while she was in a different location, with impressive detail.

When I would pick her up from school, we had a five-minute commute to pick Ledger up from daycare. This was usually the time where I'd be thinking, *what can I fix for dinner tonight?*

The first few times she mentioned "What's for dinner?" at the very moment I was thinking about it were impressive but didn't really surprise me—but this did, one afternoon after picking her up, I was thinking about making breakfast for dinner, but hadn't said anything to London about it yet. Just moments after I had decided in my head that, that was what we would be having, London said, "I don't want to have breakfast for dinner, I want mac and cheese." That, my friends, blew my mind!

My son Ledger, at just two years old, mentioned seeing a man in the corner of my bedroom one evening. I myself did not see or even sense the man. With him being just two years old I knew he truly was seeing Spirit! Because, it is very common for young children to see a full apparition, I was not surprised by this, but I was frustrated and creeped out that I myself didn't even sense the man!

Ledger is still very young and goes at a much faster pace than my daughter. He is very much an empath, always coming to the aid of another child who is hurt or sad. His telepathy skills are also starting to kick in! Just the other day, London was reading a book quietly to herself (not out loud), when Ledger walked into the kitchen (as he was playing on his iPad) and started asking me questions about snakes.

London's eyes got wide. She looked over her book and said, "Ledger, why did you ask Mom about snakes all of a sudden?" He simply said, "I don't know, the word just came into my brain." She exclaimed, "That's crazy—I just started a new chapter when you asked Mom that, and the title is 'Snakes'!

I feel that as he grows and begins to slow down a bit, his abilities will get stronger, but for now "Minecraft" video games and trains are way more important.

I'm so incredibly optimistic and excited about their abilities, I love watching them grow and I enjoy the process of watching them learn. I am grateful for the opportunity to help nurture their abilities in a way that I didn't have growing up. But I fully expect them to move to the beat of their own drum.

I want them to do what I want *you* to do: find the purpose in their lives that makes them feel complete, that sets their soul free and brings out the very best in them. I want them to find their voices in this world and shout their message from the tops of every mountain.

Chapter 11

The Bible Belt

Looking back, I think a big part of what made it so hard for me to come out of the clairvoyant closet had to do with the part of the country I lived in. Missouri is a part of the "Bible Belt" of America (due to higher church attendance and the fact that these states tend to be more socially conservative), which made it feel like this news would probably be a little harder to digest for some of my loved ones.

About two years into my career, I was set to do a mediumship event in a tiny town near Kirksville, Missouri, called Downing. A little coffeehouse had just opened up there and the owner, who attended a previous event of mine in another town, asked me if I would be willing to come there and do an event at her new shop, and so I did.

Upon my arrival, I learned that a local preacher in town had caught wind of my event and decided to take it upon himself to educate the citizens of Downing. If I remember correctly, he went door to door, handing out flyers with scripture about mediumship, and telling them that what I was doing went against God.

I know that what I do is good, that it comes from a place of love and light, and I feel confident that there are absolutely no dark energies or entities that assist me in bringing through Spirit. However, this poor guy truly believed that I was doing demonic work, and it broke my heart.

I know that at the end of the day he was simply uneducated about what I do and who I am, but I am also human, and I do not want to affect anyone in a negative way. I wonder if he had caught wind that a gay man was coming to town to have coffee—would he have reacted the same way? Would he allow a man to beat his wife in front of him, because she cheated on him, and say nothing, because the Bible said it's okay to do that? What about a man having sex with an animal? Would he be okay if one of his animals was sexually assaulted by a human? Okay, you get the picture—I'll stop.

I don't believe that all of religion is based in fear, but I do believe there are aspects of the Bible that were put into place to instill fear into the minds of Christians. Sadly, I believe that is why so many Christians are fearful and uneducated about what I do. For many, to even Google what a medium does scares them!

I am asked all the time by my students and followers, "How do you deal with the negative or uneducated people that believe you are doing the devil's work?" One of my favorite quotes (by Stefanos Tsitsipas) sums it up nicely: "I stopped explaining myself when I realized that people only understand from their level of perception." In other words, if they are not willing to educate themselves fully on a subject (in this case mediumship) before forming an opinion, then I try to "consider the source and move on." If I knew they had indeed done in-depth research, or had their own personal experiences with mediumship, and still did not believe in its validity, then I could respect them for their efforts, bless them, and agree to disagree.

I think John Edward (a medium) said it best—and covered really every kind of worldview (atheism, polytheism, monotheism, animism, etc.)—when he said, "It's okay to be skeptical, it's not okay to be cynical."

I myself was completely skeptical during my own first reading, but it is not just psychics and mediums I was and still am skeptical of—it's also lawyers, doctors, and any situation that involves risk financially, physically, or emotionally. Skepticism is a part of our ego, and our ego is in place to keep us safe from those who may be out to take advantage of us, or who don't have our best interests in mind.

If you haven't had a reading yet (assuming you have done your own research to find a psychic medium that resonates with you) I would encourage you to approach your appointment with an open mind and no expectations—

chances are you won't be disappointed that way. (that's also a good approach for

life in general!)

What I've concluded is that my experiences with Spirit encounters (as a

child), Pure Romance (having to get comfortable talking about uncomfortable

things), modeling (putting myself out there physically), pageant competitions

(being judged and getting comfortable being on a stage), losing Barb

(experiencing the same grief my clients do) and even being drugged and raped by

three men (which taught me about emotional wounds and the importance of

putting in the work to heal them, so that I could teach others about it) were all

just steppingstones. These less-than-conventional steppingstones assisted in

making it a little easier on me when the time came to step out of the clairvoyant

closet.

Here's something to think about, what do your stepping-stones look like?

When you look back on your path to purpose, (assuming you are where you want

to be in life now) do you understand a little more now why you had to go through

the things that you did? Maybe you haven't started your journey yet, if not

consider embracing each step as a gateway to something more, consider each step as a lesson, in this life, that is preparing you for your reason for being here this time around.

It took a while, and a lot of interesting situations (that's putting it lightly— this book barely scratches the surface), but I would eventually recognize that this journey was never about learning to fit in with the rest of society, something I spent over a quarter of a century trying to master. It was about accepting the fact that I was born to stand out, often in ways that have made me uncomfortable, but were also incredibly satisfying.

The Midwest (and the rest of the world) is just as thirsty for spiritual connections and guidance as I was before I discovered my purpose. They are ready for raw truth, and education from personal experiences by all different kinds of people, even metal-head mediums, because it's those kinds of people and these kinds of stories that give others hope.

They want to hear stories about psychics who don't have it all figured out. Who drive their mom's brand-new car into gas stations, get thrown out of Five Finger Death Punch concerts, and kick down 200-year-old glass doors with their boot during a psychotic mental break down (see, I told you we had only scratched the surface). They want to see the relatable side of things, not just read about how meditation can help heal all your fucking problems or what your astrological sign has in store for you for you this week.

It is the greatest honor to be one of the thousands of mediums that will help usher in light, acceptance, and healing by simply being my true, authentic self. There is no greater feeling than being a part of something bigger than who I am, while also being able to be 100 percent myself (no regrets).

I want this for you too, whatever your situation, desires, and purpose may be. I want this life for you too.

Part Two

Chapter 12

Frequently Asked Questions and Client Experiences

At the end of every show (given I have enough energy and time) I typically take a few questions from the audience. Often I am asked the same questions over and over again. Part two of this book was created to address some of the most commonly asked questions that my book has not already answered for you. I consider myself a student of the universe as well as a student of the other side; that being said, I do my best to understand and interpret what it is, exactly, that they are showing me.

I am, like all of us, constantly learning and evolving from my experiences. Most of my answers to these questions are based on what little I have been shown or told about the afterlife, whether that be through glimpses that Spirit has shown me during a reading or downloads I have received from my guides during meditation over the years. I feel incredibly honored to have had these experiences and delightfully obligated to share them with you.

Do animals that have passed on come through to you?

Yep! But that wasn't always the case. Early on it was humans only for me, and I'm sure there was a reason for that. Maybe the spirit world wanted me to only take on one thing at a time.

About two years into becoming a messenger for Spirit, I began to get a handful of pets trickling in. It took a while for me to even believe that I was in fact communicating so easily with a pet! I was a bit shocked, but not surprised (by that point nothing surprised me anymore). In the beginning I would just sense the presence and maybe the size of an animal, so I would often confuse small dogs with cats, or they might show me a panda to represent a black-and-white dog, which was also confusing, but then I slowly began to pick up on other details: wrinkly faces, a rare or special breed, or a distinct bark. Most recently, I had a basset hound howling at me during a show—talk about making it hard to concentrate!

In the early days after I started, I just assumed we mediums were all assigned to a specific type of mediumship and were meant to focus on that alone. In fact, the first couple of animals that came through, I tried to ignore! I didn't want to stray away from the human spirits that were coming through; I felt that to deviate from human spirits would go against my purpose and the reason I was given this ability.

Then one day my views on that flipped like a light switch. I was reading a married couple. After bringing through the husband's mother, sister, and brother, a dog appeared. I was only seeing the animal in black, almost like a shadow person (like the ones I saw as a child, only I could see their faces). I didn't get the color of her fur, or even the breed. But what I did get was her name, how she died, her little quirks, and a very special message for the man sitting in front of me.

The man became visibly emotional, far more emotional than he got when his own mother came through. To me, this spoke volumes; this was a type of healing that I had never even considered. To this man that dog was his everything, and the hardest part about it all was that he had to put his baby down. He was so relieved and happy to hear all was well with his pup on the other side.

From that day on I have welcomed all pets at every reading and show I do! Over the years my connection with animals in spirit has grown deeper, and it has gotten easier and easier to pick up on them! I can't always make out their breeds, colors, or names, but I can certainty feel the love and excitement they have for their owners.

Sometimes pets are even easier to talk to than humans. They are not complicated by all of the things humans are. They are clear and direct about the love they have for their moms and dads. I communicate with them telepathically, just as I do with Spirit. While I do not consider myself a pet medium, I am perfectly happy to bring them through when they show up!

Below I have included some true mediumship experiences from pet parents, through readings with yours truly, straight from their mouths.

You brought our Wolfdog Poncho through the day I met you. I asked you if my brother John was with any pets and you said he was with a pet that wasn't just an ordinary dog. He was black and huge but didn't look like a regular dog. I thought it was his Rottweiler, but you said, "No, it's longer and taller." That's when it hit me that it was Poncho. When I told you, his mother was full-blooded wolf and Dad was a Shepherd, you said, "See, I knew it wasn't your average dog!"
—Jeanie Normand

You were talking to my brother, Lee, who I miss daily, and I was pretty misty-eyed. Then you mentioned a black-and-white panda. My tears just started falling like rain. We had tragically lost the black-and-white, four-legged love of our life two months prior. She fell through the ice at our lake house. My pain was so fresh I couldn't help but cry. You said my dog was super happy with my brother. But my brother, in true fashion, said, "You didn't cry for me but you're crying for the dog!!" That made me burst out laughing.

I'm thankful they are together. Her name is Leelo and I know they are best friends. Leelo said she didn't suffer and that helped my heart to heal.

—Ruth Compton

You brought through my husky Voltaire the day he passed. I felt so guilty, but you told me he was happy, jumping around, and not in pain. You told me he sleeps in my bed with me. —Kathy Fuller

One of the first readings you did for me, I asked if you could see a dog and you said all day long you had seen a wrinkled-face dog like a Shar-pei and I said, "That was my English bulldog Sweetie!!!" Then you said, "She says she's your princess," and that was my nickname for her!! Also, I had brought my beloved Pixie with me to a reading about Cory (my son that has passed on) and I asked you if you could pick up anything from Pixie and you said she was tired. This was when her health was failing, and I knew it. I asked if you thought she had much time left and you said about six months, and it was six months later that I knew she was

ready to go and be with Cory. He had picked her out for me from a litter of eight

puppies and she was the most perfect dog I've ever had. —Cindi Watts

During one of my first sessions with you, you said my son Dustin had a dog

with him that was annoying him, then Dustin said, "You weirdos, you buried me

with the fucking dog!!" And we did put our rottweiler Macie's ashes in the casket

with him. A different session, you asked if I'd had a dream about my dad sitting

along a river with a dog. I did have that dream; you said my dad really does that,

with my dog that passed just a month before he did. —Karen Bartlett

Bringing pets through has now become one of my favorite things to do—it's like a fun furry little surprise when one pops through! I get a surge of energy from them—unlike human spirits, where I tend to feel drained after bringing them through—and who doesn't need more energy?! The companionship, love, and loyalty I have felt between an animal in spirit and their parent have honestly been some of the deepest connections I have ever experienced; as always, it is an honor.

Can you tune Spirit out?

To answer this question, I must first explain how it is that I receive information from the other side. I'm willing to bet that when most people think about what a medium experiences, you think of that movie *The Sixth Sense.* Am I right? Yeaaah...it's not like that.

Spirit is very subtle. It took 26 years before I realized I was a medium! Twenty-six years! I used to answer this question like this: "Yes, I have trained extensively out east with some of the best mediums, and through this training I have learned how to turn it on and off."

But recently, within the last couple of years, Spirit has gotten stronger and stronger—and why wouldn't they? Mediumship is after all, like a muscle—the more you work it out, the bigger it gets, or in this case, the easier it becomes to get a link (a spirit).

In the beginning of my journey, when I was just learning how to use my ability, it would have taken a very strong spirit to get my attention while I was out to dinner or grocery shopping with the kids. Now I can make a connection at the drop of the hat—but it's important for you to know, I don't see scary images of dead people walking around all the time! It is quite literally all in my head, that is the best way I know how to describe it. In fact, it typically takes me about fifteen minutes of communicating with a spirit before I get a download of what they even look like!

Communication with Spirit is much harder than communicating with the living. I take my job as a spirit speaker very seriously; you will rarely find me randomly reading someone while in line at the post office or gas station. I prefer to meditate beforehand, pray, and make my terms of communication clear with Spirit before I even begin to read someone, and these are things I can't just sit down and do in the middle of a public place. No, they're not totally necessary but they definitely make my job easier. My pre-reading process is kind of like making a phone call to schedule an appointment with your primary doctor: you can't just show up to your doctor's office without an appointment and demand to be seen right then and there. On that same note, you can just walk into a walk-in clinic without an appointment and still be seen, but it won't be by your regular doctor (the one who knows all about you, the one you feel most comfortable with), and you may have to wait longer, but at the end of the day you'll still get that antibiotic that you need to heal and move on.

The same applies to when I am out in public. If I get a message and I am unable to go through my pre-reading process, I will assess the message I am being asked to give, and if it's important or will likely lead to healing someone emotionally, I will go out of my way to get them the message, even though it makes me very uncomfortable to approach a random stranger about a subject that may or may not sit well with them. There is a fine line I have to walk, in order to show respect to both mankind and spirits.

It all makes perfect sense, when you sit back and think about it. Spirit is brilliant, they have a plan, and I believe they take into consideration each medium's needs as well as their comfort zones. Spirit is amazing at organizing life events to assist in our own individual soul's growth. I am so grateful for my amazing team of guides, and the protection of my angels. The spirit world is completely dedicated to our soul's evolution; therefore, they are dedicated to humans.

I am aware that I could get "called into work" at any moment without being paid, but I am quite alright with that. "Tuning them out" isn't in my job description; I trust they will only contact me when it's necessary.

Do you receive the same kinds of messages from your own loved ones as you do for us?

Yes! I do, but just like you I feel there is more validation behind connecting with them when I go through another medium. The validity of receiving a message from a loved one on the other side, through someone you have never met is far more powerful in my opinion. I have received many messages from my passed loved ones that have brought much peace and comfort, but I prefer to hear from them through someone else.

I like to compare it to a dentist trying to give himself a filling or a doctor trying to perform surgery on themselves. It's much easier and more effective to just sit back and let someone else bring Spirit through for a change.

Can you predict health issues?

Health predictions have always made me uncomfortable, mainly because I am in no way, shape, or form a physician. When I get a health-related vision I purposely try to be vague, just giving them the area where I feel there may be an issue, rarely ever telling the issue I am actually seeing, because I don't want to frighten someone or make them worry, especially if it is, in fact, no big deal. I feel that if I can just make you aware of the area of the problem, from there we can let the doctors do their job.

However, I will almost always tell you if I feel you may have a medical issue to be aware of. I have seen psychics and mediums literally save lives by simply making someone aware of an issue before it became fatal. To me that has been one of the absolute best things to come out of my ability.

The following are actual messages I have received over the years after having given a client my intuitive feelings about their health or the health of one of their family members. I will never claim to be a medical medium, and I will not see a client based on a health question alone, but if it comes through organically I will make sure they are aware of it.

Hey, I wanted to let you know I attended the Zoom mediumship that you did for parents that have lost a child and my daughter came through. She told you she was worried about me and showed you the diabetic sign. I was tested in August of last year so didn't think anything about it but did go get tested. I am pre-diabetic so you were right-on and hopefully we caught it and can fix it before insulin is needed! During our second in-person reading, my daughter told me to "go for it" and was referencing a big decision. I just wanted to tell you how you bringing my daughter to me and her telling me I was diabetic and have health problems saved my life. I went in for bariatric surgery in January and the doctor found all kinds of complications; the surgery was supposed to last three hours and instead lasted seven and a half. When I went back for my one-week follow-up he said my daughter saved my life: if I hadn't gotten the surgery she told me to get I wouldn't have been alive for more than a month or two!!! I can't thank you enough. Thank you, you are amazing! —Nickie Kamphaus

I want to share something with you. You visited the high school I teach at back in November and brought my dad and sister forward. You accurately conveyed many aspects of my life, literally changing my perspective on life and our world as I knew it. This came at a very difficult time in my life and the timing was surreal. I cried back in my classroom.

You also asked me if my mother had dementia or was sick. When I said she was healthy you told me she needed to see a doctor because something was wrong with her. I gave my mom the "heads up" but we both thought she was fine. In May my mom became ill and was diagnosed with stage 4 colon cancer, which is now terminal. She is now under hospice care at Luther Manor in Hannibal. My mom will pass away within days.

I want to thank you for the peace and wonder your reading has brought me during this time. I know loved ones are with us and will bring her to them in peace.

My mom just told me "Buster is here...look at him run!" Buster is her beloved childhood dog. From your gift I know he is with her, which prompted me to reach out. Thank you. You're right...everything does happen for a reason. —Erin C.

Loved the show! Also, six months ago you predicted my daughter would be pregnant soon. After suffering two miscarriages eight years ago and not being able to get pregnant since, my daughter is pregnant! —Janet Reno

Girl, you are amazing. When my mom and I saw you, you told her she needed to get her eyes checked. She went to the eye doctor today and she has very early-onset narrow angle glaucoma. Because it has been caught early there are treatment options. Had she waited; narrow angle glaucoma often leads to permanent blindness. So, THANK YOU!! You saved her eyesight! —Becky W.

Good morning! I went to your medium demonstration on July 25. At the end of your show, I walked up to thank you for your reading, and to say that I've had several friends talk with you and have loved ones come through. During our brief talk I told you I was expecting a baby in January of next year and asked if you had a sense of what the baby was. You looked at me and said, "Colton is coming."

Little did you know, Colton was actually the name we chose for our baby, and in fact was a boy. Last week we had our appointment, and we are happy to announce that your feeling was right. Baby Colton is coming January 22!!! Thank you so much for doing what you do. You're amazing. —Heidi M

Do people in your family have the same abilities that you do?

There are two parts to this question. It's important that you first understand that every medium is a psychic but not every psychic is a medium. I have been blessed with both a strong natural psychic ability as well as a mediumistic ability, but they are not the same. For decades, it seems, the terms have been used interchangeably and I am here to set the record straight for those who don't already know this.

A psychic is defined as relating to or denoting faculties or phenomena that are apparently *inexplicable* by natural laws; pertaining to or noting mental phenomena; the ability to foresee events that have not yet occurred; a person who is apparently sensitive to things beyond the natural range of perception by other humans.

A medium is defined as being in the middle of two extremes—in this case, the living world and the spirit world. This work is the practice of channeling communication between humans who have passed on physically and human beings who are still alive. Mediumship requires a very strong foundation of intuition, which is why if you are a medium you are also a psychic; as it is intuition that fuels a psychic's ability to make predictions, it is also intuition that assists you in understanding and channeling Spirit.

Before I answer this question, I think it's important to note that I did not grow up within a metaphysical environment. Everything I was ever exposed to metaphysically was through my own research. In other words, I did not grow up with hippie parents that read tarot cards and smoked weed every night. In fact, I grew up going to church and Sunday school every single Sunday. But despite my very normal upbringing, following my intuition led me to where I am today.

I believe everyone is psychic; everyone possesses the ability to use their intuition. Intuition is a natural ability we have all been given to keep us safe, to assist us in making the right choices, and to keep us from being manipulated by others (remember that last part, please). So yes, I do believe that my family members share my ability, however none of them practice professionally, and most of them don't even know they are using their psychic abilities daily to assist them in life. I enjoy getting messages from family members that start out, "Okay, why am I seeing 111" or "I had the craziest dream last night," or my all-time favorite (as we like to start off a conversation here in Missouri): "So, get this shit?!" News flash: we are all psychic!

Mediumship is a different story. I do believe a few of my immediate family members are mediums. While we have not discussed this in detail, I have grown to recognize that a few of their personal experiences have been mediumistic.

I will never push what I do on anyone; the journey to becoming a medium is a very intimate one, it must happen according to when you and you alone are ready. I have faith that their guides will lead them to an awakening and an acknowledgment of their abilities when they are ready, and when that time comes it would be an honor to assist them in their unfolding and education, should they choose to work with me.

If I want to talk to a certain loved one on the other side, is it guaranteed that they will come through? If not, why?

The simple answer is no. I can say that I have never personally not been able to bring a particular spirit through when they were requested by name and/or relationship, but that's not to say that there won't be a day when this happens. Anything is possible.

The clarity of the connection between myself and a particular spirit is a lot like when you meet someone for the first time: you are usually either put off by them, cool with them, or you get along famously and crave more interaction with that individual. The same goes for Spirit and myself—when the conversation flows and we get along well, the strength of that connection allows me to deliver deeper, clearer messages. If our connection is poor—which can be due to a number of things that include how I am feeling that day, my energy and/or stress level (which is why on days that I read I am dedicated to meditation and putting myself in a stress-free environment), as well as how the sitter is feeling, how open (or closed off) they are to receiving information from Spirit, and how they themselves feel physically at the time of their reading.

The few times when I have had a problem getting a clear, flowing connection happened because I pushed myself to read for someone when I did not feel my best (I have since learned that it's much better to cancel, even if it upsets my client, than to try to make a connection that could result in a less-than-stellar reading) or when my client was not opened to receiving any other kind of information than what they had specifically asked their loved one to bring through.

While we are on this subject, please don't ask your loved one to tell me something specific so you know it's really them. Remember, they may hear and understand exactly what you want, but them getting me to understand that is a whole different ball game. Please just allow the reading to unfold naturally. I will pick up on the things I can understand but putting unnecessary energetic stress on the medium and your loved one like that could result in a negative experience. Trust that your loved one will find a way to make sure you know that they are in fact communicating with you.

While struggling to make a connection is a rare phenomenon for me, it does happen. But I take a genuine interest in what messages Spirit wants me to pass on; I do my best to be patient with them and I put in the time and effort before every reading to make myself absolutely available, and I think they appreciate this. I believe these efforts have made the rapport between myself and any given spirit of love and light quite special!

Do you receive futuristic/psychic messages for yourself or only for other people?

I do, all the time! But just as I described previously about getting messages from loved ones, it's always more impactful and meaningful to receive them through someone else. You yourself may have paid for a psychic reading, seeking an answer as to how a situation would unfold, only to find that what the psychic told you, you already knew. Hey, don't blame us because you didn't listen to your own intuition!

All jokes aside, one of my favorite personal downloads came in June of 2019. I was on my way to a show in Columbia, Missouri, when I heard a song that made me emotional. Through tears, I asked my guides if I was ever going to fall in love again. In that moment I heard the answer in my head. They said, *Yes, he isn't quite ready for you yet, you will know him by his mark, his name will start with a M, you will meet him in the dead of winter, he will have distinct teeth, look for the number 22 for confirmation, you will have to make a very hard decision, and you will not be compatible astrologically.*

That last one was very important for them to throw in there, as they knew I would have avoided a man of his sign had they not told me this beforehand. I felt a wave of peace wash over me; I knew that this would come to fruition.

In February of 2020 (dead of winter), I met Mathew (his name will start with an M). The first picture I saw of him caught my eye because he had an anti-possession/pentagram tattoo on his chest (you will know him by his mark). It made me look twice—I was like, no fucking way! Mat is a Cancer, a sign known to be less than compatible with a Gemini (you will not be compatible astrologically).

That psychic download from my guides allowed me to feel confident about stepping into a new relationship—something that, while I desired it, I was also very leery of. The jury is still out on the "very hard decision" part, so there is still an element of mystery to the relationship to this day (but I kind of love that).

On our very first date, I got up from the table to excuse myself; I was feeling Spirit deeply in the restaurant and I felt very overwhelmed. When I came back from the bathroom, Mat said, "Check this out" (I had told him about the download I had before we met, so he knew this would mean something to me). He slid the check from our meal over to me, and the total was $22.22 (look for the number 22 for confirmation). Oh, and yes, he has teeth crowding and I love that too (he will have very distinct teeth). He's quite handsome—my guides did well!

Today we are going on year four, we both have full custody of our children; we

both have one girl and one boy, for a total party of six! We are dedicated to

putting our children first in all aspects of our relationship and that's one of the

things I love most about him.

This is the very first picture I ever saw of him. I realize it's not the best quality, but it was important

for me to show you exactly what I first saw. So handsome! Oh, and to your right is my favorite picture of us!

Photo credit to Pamela Hoth of Pamela Michelle Photography.

What do you mean when you say, "They are showing

me my sign for...?"

I call the Images Spirit shows me "spirit symbology," which is a collection of signs and symbols that are as unique to a medium and the spirit world as your very own fingerprint!

In the beginning, mediumship was very hard for me to navigate. I found myself absolutely drained after just one reading, but that was because I hadn't yet created a dialect with Spirit. Therefore, it was taking a tremendous amount of energy for me just to get one small detail, and often that one small detail still had to be interpreted by myself or my client, if it wasn't obvious immediately.

If you can, imagine being deaf, and unable to communicate with anyone. It would be absolutely exhausting to try to communicate with others without sign language, or at the very least a pen and paper! Just as sign language was created as a form of communication for those that cannot hear, spirit symbology was created to assist a medium when channeling Spirit, in lieu of being able to use the physical body for communication. Spirit symbology allows a medium to quickly understand some of the most commonly discussed topics between Spirit and their loved ones.

About three months into my mediumship journey, during a reading the spirit I was communicating with showed me a lake. My first thought was vacation (I have literally no clue why vacation came to mind, since visiting a lake is not my idea of a vacation). Instead of saying "I'm seeing a lake" like most people would, I asked if vacation was important to her or late husband. She said, "He died while we were on vacation."

After the reading I remember thinking, *wait a minute, the last time I saw a lake in a reading* [several weeks prior] *it led to talk of vacation for my client.* I wondered if it was related.

The next time I had a reading that involved me seeing a lake, I again asked if going on a vacation or traveling was important to my sitter or their passed loved one. She said, "I am leaving tomorrow with the rest of our family to spread my brother's ashes in the ocean. We're renting a house on the beach in Florida and celebrating his life, he died in Florida and loved the ocean."

What I was doing to find the meaning behind the lake was called mind mapping (if you recall, I mentioned this in a previous chapter). I was shown something easy to understand, something very basic, that quickly made me think of something else—it made me think of what my own mind associates with this picture. That's when it clicked for me: I had heard other mediums talk about their "symbols" but had no clue what they really meant.

From that point on, I realized that if Spirit shows it to me more than once, it's now a part of our special dialect. Spirit is constantly adding new symbols to my legion of words. Through the use of mind mapping, Spirit and I have created hundreds of symbols that assist me in interpretating messages, much quicker and with better accuracy.

Why are numbers so important to you?

Hold on to your seat, this is a long one—but only because I am so passionate about numbers and their connection with Spirit! However, as much as I love numbers, I stink at math; if it hadn't been for my high school boyfriend's mother being my math teacher, I don't think I would have graduated!

Numbers speak to me in a special way, and I love turning them into words. Numbers are the Universe's and Spirit's quickest way to get our attention and to help us make connections in life that can guide us toward enlightenment, closure, and even our true life's purpose. Just one number can bring me the validation I need personally, to believe and know that I have made a link with a specific loved one for you.

I can't remember how or exactly when numerology became such an integral part of my ability, but I do feel it is the quickest and easiest way for me to prove to myself that I have who I say I have! If you think about it, every single person on this planet comes into the world with a specific set of numbers and leaves with a specific set of numbers. Think about the last baby that was born in your family, the date in which they entered our world, the time, how much they weighed—the same goes for when we transition back home, we have a time of death, a date of death, how many years we were alive, and so on. Numbers are facts, they are how we measure everything, so it just seems fitting to me that I ask Spirit for a number upon meeting them—so many messages and so much confirmation can come from just one number!

If you attend one of my events, you will view a slideshow before we begin that explains how I work with Spirit, shows reviews from those who have been read, tells you to expect cussing (sorry not sorry), and most importantly to "know your numbers!" This means that if you have a loved one that was born or passed on the 10th of any month, or in the month of October, and I am seeing the number 10 (the tenth month of the year being October), then I may be looking to connect with you—so knowing the important dates before attending is imperative!

However, numbers are not only linked to death dates or birthdates of a passed loved one; in fact, often they have nothing to do with dates at all. Spirit has allowed me to bring up numbers that anchor the living to their departed in so many cool ways. I once brought through a son named Joe for my client Angela; he kept showing me #22, over and over again—it turned out his mother connected deeply with that number because it was his football jersey number. Since his passing, seeing that number made her feel closer to him. When I brought up that number in particular, she knew, without a doubt it was him!

There are also tons of other ways Spirit can use a number to make a quick, accurate, and profound connection as evidence of their existence. Think of a fireman's company number, or a policeman's badge number, the number of children a woman had, a racetrack number, the number of a favorite famous sports player, a significant and particular number of collected items, a parking spot number, an anniversary or number of years someone was sober before passing, a flight number, or maybe in the case of 420, they were just a cool ass, weed loving hippie. The possibilities are endless for numeric connections and I am so glad that my guides have chosen this as one of my strongest methods of spirit communication.

But I don't just use numbers to communicate with Spirit, I receive many of my psychic downloads through numbers as well. In 2018, while driving to an event, I had a vision. It was simple: just the number 19, accompanied by the physical feeling of fear, panic, and a pain in my chest. Assuming this was a foreboding date of some kind, I mentioned to my Facebook followers that all should steer clear of any events happening on or around the 19th of any month for the next few months, just to be on the safe side. Keep in mind, this vision came at a time when our country was encountering one mass shooting after another. I felt that the number 19 event would be something that affected hundreds if not thousands of people.

In the months following this vision, several tragedies did ensue on the 19th, or involved the number 19. However, I still felt like it was only the beginning, it just didn't feel over; it didn't feel like what was supposed to happen had happened yet. At the time of my vision, I had never even heard of Covid-19 (not a big news-watcher, don't have the time and it's just too negative for me) and neither had most of my followers on Facebook—at least, looking back it didn't appear that way, as no one mentioned it as a possibility when I posted it!

It wasn't until March of 2020 that I realized why I felt the way I did whenever I saw the number 19: that sharp pain in my chest, feeling like I couldn't breathe—even the physical feeling I felt matched the symptoms of Covid-19! That was around the time the US started to shut down to avoid the spread of Covid.

I am a firm believer, after all of my personal experiences, that we are all connected by numbers, and I hope that from reading this particular part of the book you will begin to pay more attention to the numbers around you and the meaning behind them!

There is one last story I'd like to share involving a few powerful numbers, which ended up creating an extremely close bond that I still have to this day with a former client. In fact, I now call this woman Mom!

It was a cold, rainy night in January 2017 and still very early in my professional career when I was standing in front of my microwave, spacing out while watching a cup of hot cocoa go round and round, waiting for the beep. Just before it was done I heard in a manly voice "Britney!"—loud and clear, like someone was urgently trying to get my attention.

I walked back into the living room. Assuming Andrew had said my name, I said "What?" He was the only person awake in the house; the kids were sound asleep. He looked at me like I was nuts, laughed, and said, "I didn't say anything." I said, "You're fucking with me" he said, "No, I'm not!"

Beeeeeeeeeeep, the microwave went off. I walked back into my dimly lit kitchen, completely perplexed. When I "hear" Spirit it is in my head—in other words, it is not audible to other people, and it is not loud, but this was. There is a very distinct difference, so I knew this was clearly someone in the room saying my name, in my mind that could only be Andrew.

I brought my cocoa back into the living room and settled in to watch a movie. While the previews played I quickly flipped through my phone, I gasped, as I saw that Andrew's favorite art teacher Pat Kerns had lost her son! I didn't know Pat personally; Andrew had introduced me to her a couple times at art shows we attended but that was it. She seemed very nice and was so sweet to him.

This news came moments after audibly hearing my name. For a fleeting second I had an overwhelming knowing that it was Thadd, Pat and Bill Kerns' son—he was the one that said my name in the kitchen. I had never met Thadd and didn't even know what he looked like. Hardly knowing Pat and Bill myself, it was hard for me to fathom that this random person in spirit would reach out to me—and if it was him, why only say my name, why not give me a message to pass along to them?

I told Andrew that I knew I would read Pat one day. He looked at me like I was crazy. They posted that there would be a celebration of life for Thadd at one of the local art galleries in town. I told Andrew he should go, but unfortunately he had to work on two clients that had already planned to take off work and were traveling to him. So, I decided that I would go for him and pay our respects.

I walked in and immediately felt out of place. I knew almost no one there; I didn't grow up in Hannibal, and Thadd was over a decade older than me. I saw Pat standing up by a huge picture of Thadd. He looked beautiful in this picture, and it looked like there was a light above Pat shining down on her—she looked heavenly (come to think of it, there probably was a light shining down on her, it was an art gallery).

I approached her and said, "Andrew couldn't make it today, he had to work, but I wanted to extend our condolences on his behalf, you mean a great deal to him." She smiled and said thank you. She told me something about the kind of artist Andrew was. We smiled, I hugged her, and then I left.

About six months later, Pat reached out to me on Facebook Messenger, she said, "I'd like to know more about your angel messages." I had been waiting for that message. I explained how they worked: I told her I read from my home and we set up an appointment.

A few days later she arrived at my front door. I showed her into my dining room, and I began to connect with Thadd. Pat asked me if I saw any specific number, and I said, "Yes, he keeps showing me 11/11." She smiled and said, "That was his birthday." As you may know, 11:11 is also a very special synchronicity to see and is often associated with being a sign from Spirit.

She then asked me to ask him when her birthday was. I felt a strong sense of confusion and then he showed me 11/24, then flashed back to 11/23, then showed me 11/24 again. I explained this to her, and she laughed out loud. She said, "He could never remember the exact date of my birthday; he would often assume it was the 24th when in fact it was the 23rd of November." I could tell by the look in her eyes that, in that moment, she knew he was there with us.

She then asked me if I could tell her how much money he had loaned someone. He showed me $10,000. She said, "Yes! That's exactly the amount we thought!"

While her reading had many more incredible moments, it was the numbers that brought her the proof she needed. From that moment on, Pat and I formed a deep mother-daughter bond that has gotten us both through many hard days. She introduced me to Thadd's partner Liza, and she and I also grew close after I brought him through for her. The three of us text daily, and it's rare for a day to go by that one of us doesn't send an "I love you" at exactly 11:11 to our group message thread. I have no doubt that Thadd was responsible for this connection.

How do you handle people who feel that what you do is dark or negative?

This question in particular (while very loaded) is actually what led me to write this book and is the reason behind the title *Brave*. Coming out publicly as a psychic and medium was one of the hardest things I have ever done in my life, mainly because those who live by the Bible believe that mediumship and psychic abilities in anyone other than the prophets of the Bible are associated with evil and the devil himself.

I find that viewpoint particularly hypocritical for many reasons, but without writing another book on my feelings about this subject I will give it to you straight and simple. The Bible condones bigamy, cannibalism, incest, slavery, genocide, beating women, having sex with your children, rape, and bestiality, just to name a few, and it reviles women, mediums, psychics, lesbians, and gays. If you are going to worship a book like that, my concern doesn't lie in how you feel about who I am or what I do for a living, my concern is for you. After all, aren't Christians supposed to be loving, accepting, nonjudgmental beings? That is the exact opposite of what I have seen from *some* of the Christians that have sent me long messages on Facebook, through email, and even going so far as to mail letters to my office, warning me of a fiery hell if I don't repent with them immediately.

And for the record, not once in any of the thousands of readings I have done have I ever encountered anyone from the other side that says they are from hell or looks like they are on fire. Nor have I ever come into contact with a dark being, demon, or any other negative entity (and trust me, I am the most sensitive person I know; I know when I see a wolf in sheep's clothing). If hell does exist, I don't want any part of it!

But here's my question: why can't we worship the same God with different views? I don't believe there needs to be a separation between religion and spiritualism. I also do not believe that all of religion is based in fear, but I do believe there are aspects of the Bible that were put into place by man thousands of years ago to instill fear in the minds of Christians, in order to gain and keep control of them. While I don't feel that the Church "controls" people today, I do feel that was the main purpose behind many of the things that were written in the Bible long ago.

The readings I do take time away from my children and family, they require me to set aside my own life to become an instrument for Spirit. These readings are work, a lot of work, they leave me feeling depleted, and sometimes physically sick. Missing persons and cold cases, are all done for free and always at the drop of a hat which can be very inconvenient, I also wish to always remain anonymous,

I don't get some grand reward, there is no demon giving me eternal beauty or life-long health to help other people. Aside from keeping food on the table what is in it for me? Where is this dark motivator so many speak of in the Bible?

I'll tell you what I do know, every single one of these sessions has provided a great deal of peace, proof, guidance, and healing to those on the receiving end. These readings have saved so many, medically, financially, mentally, and emotionally. I have seen a reading keep a mother from committing suicide, help someone forgive themselves after years of self-torture and guilt, save someone's eyesight and breath life back into so many suffering in anguish. I struggle to see how this work can be anything but good, and right, and beautiful—these are messages of love, light, and hope.

With that being said, I think it is important for me to tell you that I do believe in God. But I do not believe that God rules over us with fear and the threat of eternal damnation. I feel this fear was created by man through the Bible in order to control people, to make sure they stayed in line, paid their taxes, and obeyed the often-cruel laws set out before them so long ago. What's sad, is this book that is so worshipped condones the deaths of so many innocent lives as well: the floods, the Egyptian firstborn sons, the Witch Trials, just to name a few.

It's truly sickening, I sometimes wonder if Bible-followers would treat any other book about meaningless deaths, war, slavery, and rape with the same devotion?

I believe God is a positive Source of connection for all beings, alive and passed. This Source is a helpful, beautiful being that is willing to assist those who want to help themselves and reward those who are kind to others. I believe in a God that promotes love, harmony, and peace. I don't believe that God is responsible for absolutely everything that happens (as some Christians believe)— if that's the case, why would he condone rape or murder? What is his reasoning behind taking the life of an innocent child?

I believe the Universe and God work hand in hand: I call the Universe God's secretary. The Universe makes sure that we are in the right places at the right times, according to our own karmic actions and previously signed soul contracts. We may not have any say in the bad things that happen to us at the hands of others, but I do believe that God's secretary, the Universe will make sure that her sister, Karma, takes care of those morally misguided individuals.

I believe we are spiritual beings having a human experience, not the other way around. The purpose of a soul contract is to teach our souls to be more Christlike, or to ascend (to undergo a series of spiritual transformations and become enlightened by each life lived on Earth). Essentially, I believe it is our souls mission to learn how to be kind, loving, accepting, and forgiving at all times, through the experiences that we have had here on Earth (and yes, I most definitely believe in reincarnation). Jesus Christ is one of the world's most influential and inspiring ascended masters. The outcasts of society—the prostitutes, the sick, the sinners, the ones others assumed would be dammed to hell for their actions—flocked to Jesus because he made them feel special, safe, and loved. He accepted each and every one of them for who they were; his love and acceptance motivated them, just as his love for us motivates me. This proves that love and peace far outweigh the concept of fear and the idea of eternal damnation.

I'd like to share with you something beautiful that happened about two years ago, involving Jesus. While vacationing in Florida with my dear friend Chantelle, we both experienced his power; to say it was magical would be an understatement. We were lying by the pool under a giant umbrella, watching our children splash and play in the pool, when I told her I was feeling compelled to work with Jesus. I had been getting signs from him all month and the need to connect with him was growing. She said, "Then do it, what are you waiting for?"

I said, "I'm scared, because of what's been written in the Bible about mediums—what if he doesn't accept me or wants to change me?! I am happy with who I am, and I am happy with where I stand spiritually and religiously."

She said, "Jesus didn't write the Bible, and he was prophetic, just like you are—you share a common ground. He's an amazing person, and I think you will love him."

I said, "I already do love him. I believe in his story, and I'm grateful for him and the journey he went through. I'm just scared because of what I was taught in church as a child."

I must have forgotten that Jesus himself was considered an outcast; I take refuge in that fact in my weakest of moments, when I am reading those horrible emails or trying to stand up for my work while being torn down by those that pity me for my life path. His journey taught me that even if you don't understand why or what you are being asked to do, even if you can't physically see something or make sense of it scientifically, if it feels right to you, if it feels like you are being guided by the divine you should move forward with conviction and faith.

I told Chantelle, "I guess I let the fear that came from the Bible, and the assumption that Jesus may look down on me because of what has been written, cloud my ability to start working with him. It just goes to show you exactly how much control fear alone can have on you."

Just as I finished saying this, my son (six at the time and an avid lover of planes) shouted, "Mommy, Mommy, look up in the sky—that plane is writing words, what do they say?!"

Chantelle and I got up from under the umbrella and this is what we saw...

Kissimmee Florida Resorts, April 2022

A plane in the sky was writing "Praise Jesus." It was such an incredible moment in both our lives. I knew in that moment that Jesus, was there, confirming everything we felt and, most importantly, everything we said.

So, I ask anyone reading this book, should you see mediumship and psychic abilities as evil, why can't we both at least worship the same God, but have different views on how and from where we worship? I choose to believe that God is not attached to the darkness of the Bible, or what happened thousands of years ago to thousands of innocent people, that was man's doing. God is someone I look to for strength and connection with the divine, with my guides, and my angels. Jesus is someone I look to for inspiration, acceptance, and most importantly, guidance. I will continue to lead a life of love, as a fearless, heavy metal–loving badass, promoting peace, the occasional curse word, and kindness in Jesus's name. Amen.

Do your tattoos have specific meanings, and if so what are they?

I get asked this question quite often, so I thought I would address each one for you right here! When I was 15 years old I remember watching a biography show on Jenna Jameson (yes the porn star) and just being completely floored by all she had gone through. At the end of the show, they talked a bit about her iconic "heartbreaker" booty tat. I fell in love with it, and I knew right then and there I wanted that to be my first tattoo! I can't explain exactly what drew me to it, other than I just loved the idea and location. At just 19, that particular tattoo would eventually lead to my marriage of the artist that did it, who would become the father of my children. Hindsight 20/20 (no pun intended), I wouldn't change a thing and I still love the tattoo to this day!

I wouldn't get another tattoo for more than six years. I always laughed at those who said ink was an addiction; being married to a tattoo artist, I heard it almost daily, but I never felt that way. For me tattoos have always been a way to express who I am to the world without having to say a word. Therefore, each tattoo I have has meaning, each has been intentional and especially thought-out—no crazy drunken tattoo stories here.

The next tattoo I acquired came about because of the gratitude I experienced when I became a mother. The word "Blessed" spelled out in Old English on my right upper thigh was a reminder that I have been blessed with the most amazing role in this life, and that is to be a mother. Because my daily life is often planned out right down to the very minute, I had the letter "B" positioned on my forearm at the same time, as an eloquent reminder to just "be" present in life.

The half-mandala wrist wrap was the next design, and it came about just before I got pregnant with my son, Ledger, in 2015. It serves as a reminder of how important balance and peace is, especially after stepping into motherhood. It also has a lotus flower inside of it to remind me that just like the lotus, I, too, am resilient and strong. After Ledger was born in 2016 I had his name tattooed on my left hand and my daughter London's name tattooed on my right hand. They love those tattoos so much. Anytime we are going somewhere that requires them to hold my hand they always make sure they get the hand that has *their* name on it.

The angel wing on my left forearm is for all the loved ones in Spirit I have brought through and will continue to bring through. It is situated in a way that others can easily see it, because in my mind it serves as a badge of honor, commitment, and loyalty to the spirit world as well as my sitters.

To date, the only tattoo I have ever gotten with a friend is the crescent moon behind my right ear. My friend Holly (you remember Holly, the nurse) and I got them together. For me it symbolizes new beginnings, as it was during that time that I was just starting to explore my abilities and really allow myself to accept who I was as a medium.

Did Andrew still do my tattoos even after our divorce? Of course, he's an amazing artist, and the third eye tattoo on my right wrist was the next tattoo he did for me. Knowing my profession, one might assume that's the meaning behind it. While that is not an incorrect statement, there is a little more to the story. I have a rare condition called Kienbock's, where the blood supply to one of the small bones in my wrist, called the lunate—the only bone in the body named after the moon, because of its shape—has been interrupted. I had to have a proximal row carpectomy, which is the removal of one of the two rows of small bones in the wrist, done in 2018, and it left a large scar on my wrist and upper hand. I looked at this as a great opportunity for some new ink! I chose the third eye piece to cover it as a reminder to trust that I had been given the ability as a seer for a reason, and that I should always trust myself. It reminds me to never second-guess my choices and ability.

Like the moon, we all go through phases. I wanted to be reminded of this daily, therefore I got a set of moon phases on my upper left arm; I also just really love the artistic vision of this tattoo, it's both delicate and bold.

The next two tattoos I received are the only two I got from an artist other than Andrew. I have GEMINI under my moon phase tattoo as a statement and claim to my birth sign—as I am, a proud, loud, and wild Gemini! I would collect one more tattoo from Adam Fenton at Threshold of Pain, though I am sure I will get more from him in the future, he's a class act and an awesome artist! He tattooed the symbols of the four elements on the back of my upper arm. Earth, Air, Fire, and Water: this tattoo reminds me that we are all working with the exact same elements in life. No one is above them; we are all connected in this way, and I feel it is a beautiful testament to all that our mother the Earth provides for us.

My latest and probably most meaningful tattoo is that of Archangel Michael on my right bicep. He is my protector; he has never let me down. I feel extremely connected to God's right-hand angel. I chose an image of him with a cross as a testament to my faith in God and Jesus Christ.

Why metal and rock music and not something more calming?

Well, that's just it, metal music is calming to me! It's no secret that music is mankind's most magnificent creation, it has amazing healing properties no matter what form it's in, it's also an incredible coping mechanism! Don't get me wrong, I appreciate all music and I have grown fonder of some country artists over the years. Perhaps it's unusual for some to find comfort and peace in metal and rock 'n' roll music, but not for me. it is my safe place, the one place where I can let it all out, and really just be myself.

I grew up listening to it with my dad, metal music inspires excitement, motivation, and a zest for life! I love the idea of getting my crowds pumped up before a show, in the same way that I am backstage—I feel like it brings a certain level of intensity to the energy of the room that just can't be matched by anything else. Metal is the one form of music where I feel the artists hold absolutely nothing back, they go all in with their emotions, they are giving every ounce of raw passion, and every bit of energy they have to you, their audience, and that's something I can identify with. It was suggested that I leave these last two questions out, as they are not as important as the rest of the information in this book, and I understand that, but my tattoos and love for rock music are both a huge part of my identity. Not to mention they are two things I get asked about often by, you, and you are one of the biggest reasons I wrote this book! They are two things that really set me apart from the rest of the world of mediums, and once again, that is something I am proud of. I want to lead by example, I want to embrace my uniqueness, and share it with those who care, and I want you to do the same.

Chapter 13

Conclusion

As of October 2023, I have done more than seven thousand readings, and nearly three hundred live-audience events, and it never fails: I am often just as surprised as the people sitting in front of me when evidence is delivered from Spirit. Over the years I have received so many beautiful notes, not just of appreciation, but countless testimonies from newfound believers, people whose lives have been changed radically by mediumship alone. I have decided to share some of these notes of gratitude and healing with you. I am not sharing these out of vanity, but instead, hoping to inspire you, and to further prove the importance of psychic science and mediumship. I want to show you what a difference you can make in someone else's life by simply being honest with yourself, taking a leap of faith, and believing in who you are, and whatever purpose you were put on this planet to serve.

My husband and I had very affordable tickets to a Zoom demonstration of Britney's with several other people in attendance. We had the absolute experience of a lifetime.

When Britney started describing the specific circumstances around our loved one's passing, we identified ourselves as fitting the details. From there on out, we were blown away. Our loved one brought up every single thing that I know she would have brought up, and the way that Britney described her stature and personality fit our loved one TO A "T"!! It was exactly like hearing from our loved one when she was at her absolute happiest and having fun.

The chance to hear from her was the reason we were there, and she said the most important things we needed to hear. It was amazing.

Britney could not have known any of those little details that she did not get from us. Britney would say something amazing, then we would fill her in with more details so she could better interpret was she was receiving. And then we'd get surprised again! To have this gift we were given, was a beautiful blessing. Thank you so, so much!! —Christina Scherman-Gander, Charlotte, NC

I met with Britney on January 15, 2020. My wife had purchased this reading for me after a similar experience she had with a medium recently. As a middle-aged adult, I have always believed in mediums and their abilities to connect with *our loved ones that have passed on, but to some extent seeing is believing. Britney exceeded all my expectations for the reading. Although slightly nervous walking into Britney's office, she was quick to make me feel comfortable and relaxed with her outgoing personality. She explained her gift and how she uses it to bring messages through. Once we established who I was hoping to connect with, the reading started.*

My mother passed in 1993 and I was somewhat worried that with such a long time between her death and now that she may not be able to come through. I was surprised with how quickly Britney connected to both my mother and my father, who had passed in 2014. The facts and memories that Britney communicated could only be known by myself and my deceased parents. Prior to my reading I had grabbed a cross necklace that my mother had given me as a present for my high school graduation many years ago and placed it in the pocket of my jeans where it was not visible. I had not worn the cross in many years as it stayed on the nightstand next to my bed. At the end of my reading Britney acknowledged that she had asked my mother if she had anything else to communicate before we finished. Britney then said to me, "The cross." The hair on my neck stood straight up and my eyes filled with tears, even though I said I was not going to cry.

Britney was also able to connect with a great friend that I had lost in 1992 to a senseless act of violence. I had carried guilt around with me since his passing as I was not with him the night the incident took place. I always thought I could have stopped it from happening or altered his plans that night. Obviously, I had not told Britney how my friend died and there was no way she could have known, due to how long ago the event occurred. So, when she said to me, "He wants me to talk about the murder, because it's a big deal to you," I felt the years of guilt and grief leave my body. There was nothing I could have done to prevent it and he was glad I was not involved.

There are so many other messages I could write about from my reading. Britney truly has a gift that was shared with me and the results changed my life. What a blessing. —H.L., Hannibal, MO

[This reading] forever changed my life. I was at a point where I was so overwhelmed with all life in general. Mainly stemming from losing my father... As I drove home after our session I was so happy. I felt so much peace. Since then, my life has changed drastically. In such a positive way. All of my friends have heard my experience and are amazed. I hope they take the step to meet you too!

Thank you Britney, for helping me find the peace I needed to move on just a little. What you do truly changes lives, gives people peace, answers that weighed heavy on their hearts for so many years, and enough hope for the future that it's okay to keep moving forward and not feel guilty about it. You are such a blessing in my life. I can't wait to share this experience with my mother tomorrow. — Heather M., Kirksville, MO

[The reading] proved to me my Baby is still around me. But the person you are touched my soul. You continued to reach out to me. You didn't have to. But you did. It showed me that your gift is something you truly consider a gift from God. #Heaven — Angela C., Kansas City, MO

The best validation for me was when my son led you to my purse. Before the reading I placed something of his in my purse. I told no one and left my purse on the floor during the reading. Parker led you right to it. No way you could have known about that. — Donna R., Quincy, IL

I want to give Britney a super huge thank you! For an incredible reading today! Britney, your incredible gift brought warmth and smiles to my wife and I while we

go through these tough times! I highly recommend your services. You're AWESOME!

I wish I would have asked more questions! But my whole family is amazed! First thing you said to me in the lounge: "Who is Ryan?" Amazing! Then all the other messages from my dear son totally validated the reading. And the fact that you flagged us down as we were outside the building because you had so much more to share about my boy! God bless you, Britney! Sorry for blowing up your page with so many messages, I'm just so touched by what you gave us!—KW, Sullivan, MO

I lost my husband seven weeks ago and after talking to this amazing woman I am finally feeling at peace.... I am so very grateful to have met you and I literally could have sat and talked to you all night. I want to thank you from the bottom of my heart for helping me and I can't wait to be able to sit and talk to you again. Thank you again. —Carrie, Ursa, IL

THANK YOU SO MUCH!! I slept until 6:45 this a.m., first time I've slept past 4 a.m. since my husband passed. You answered so many questions and brought so much peace.... I look forward to meeting with you again.... —Deb, Hull, IL

Skepticism implies unwillingness to believe without conclusive evidence. That was me...heavy on the "was." After a tragic accident took the life of my 23-year-old son Keegan in February 2015, I had a few dreams with him in them but that was my only contact. There was a phone reading (that I was not part of— more skepticism) with Britney approximately two years ago.

Fast forward to the summer of 2021, when I learned that during that phone reading, Britney referred to Keegan's girlfriend at the time of his passing by her first name. The girlfriend was a fairly new relationship and there is no way Britney would have known her name unless there was something to this. There are millions of names out there, it could not have been a lucky guess.

September of 2021, Britney conducted a group reading in Springfield, Illinois. A ticket was bought for me, so I went. As soon as Britney saw me in the hallway, she was able to identify who I was and she said, "He has been waiting for this, he is ready to go." The reading began in the room and within minutes, she was able to tune in with Keegan. She related things that nobody in the world would have known but Keegan and I. So, I know it was real and that day was the closest I have felt to him for the past almost seven years. She even brought up our cat that had just passed away three weeks prior, saying that Keegan wanted me to know that "your damn cat is here."

Britney gave me hope that I will someday see Keegan again. Britney, I appreciate you and want you to know that you brought this dad some comfort and peace that day...and even a few laughs. —Adam W., Springfield, IL

I've crossed the threshold of my fears—and on the other side was who I was always meant to be. I hope, if you are not already living out your true passion in life, that this book kicks your ass into gear and gives you the motivation to move forward with your dreams.

My wish for you, after reading about my journey thus far, is that you stop denying yourself of what your intuition is so boldly begging you to pay attention to. Even if you fear that what you actually want to do is not practical enough, according to everyone else around you, follow that path anyway! If there is one thing I have learned since I started this adventure, it is that this life is fleeting, and we were all sent here to serve a greater purpose than existence alone. We all have a gift or an ability that is meant to change, improve, or assist humankind in some way. We are here to make a difference and you cannot do that by being silent.

I'd like to leave you with one last thing. If you would, please take a moment and ask yourself something for me: "Am I being honest with myself?" If you are unsure of what your purpose might be, look at your emotional and mental wounds, (maybe even your physical ones) figure out how to heal them, and then teach others with those same wounds how to heal themselves.

Your purpose may not be something you get paid for, but I can promise you, once you discover it, you will make a difference in this world and you will find the deepest sense of gratification and satisfaction within.

I hope this book gives you the courage to break through your walls of insecurity and ego and heal the emotional wounds that are holding you back! Tell your ego to go fuck itself, find your inner badass, and step into a happier, more fulfilling life. It is important for you to remember that there is strength, and courage, and power in vulnerability. The ability to not let other people define you is a gift—open that gift up and use it!

Find your voice and you will find peace. Being brave is just doing something you are afraid of. Some bravery requires an emotional suit of armor instead of a physical one, so suit up, bitches! It's time to get uncomfortable! Never forget, you can't be brave if you're never scared.

"For there is always light if only we're brave enough to see it, if only we're brave enough to be it." —Amanda Gorman

Made in the USA
Monee, IL
31 October 2023

45531371R00121